ISIS - Afrík

Akkadía Ford

CAPALL BANN PUBLISHING

ISIS - Afrikan Queen

©1999 Akkadia Ford

ISBN 186163 066 2

Cover design by Paul Mason
Internal illustrations & cover picture by Akkadia Ford

Published by:

Capall Bann Publishing
Freshfields
Chieveley
Berks
RG20 8TF

Contents

Synopsis

Isis is a majestic and powerful ancient Goddess-form; one who combines the insights obtained from thousands of years of a practical and high religion within the ancient Egyptian mysteries, with solutions to the deepest questions and needs of a modern mind.That Her re-emergence within the Twentieth Century has occurred at the same time that the degradation of the natural world escalates, is no coincidence; for the 'Old Gods' always return when they are needed and Isis has always been a Goddess who cares deeply about the Earth - for it is Her Throne - embodying the powers of nature and renewal.

The primary intention of Isis, Afrikan Queen is to reinstate an understanding of the Goddess' ancient powers and accompanying symbols. It is designed as a 'working book' and whether familiar with the Egyptian Mysteries, or awakening to their power, a comprehensive means of establishing and maintaining a sacred practise under the auspices of Isis is included. The practitioner is led towards integrating the relationship of the macrocosmic structure of the Egyptian realms and the microcosm which the Temple Service and its servitors, both in the daily and annual rites represented.

Background information to enable a clear view of who Isis was and what Her powers were within the Egyptian system is provided : the tools (hieroglyphic, animal forms and attendant symbolism/practical applications, ritual objects/meanings and related lore) are provided, to enable a working relationship to

1

be established for the new practitioner and additional insights and new ways of approaching Her for those already established in their practise.

An annual Festival Cycle is included, which brings the theoretical understanding of Isis into a practical format, easily adapted to either solo or group working. It is within this Cycle that the deep renewal which the Mysteries of Isis enable, are experienced within each aspirant. The potential of the individual practitioner is further explored through the ancient Temple rite of the "Incubation Sleep "(the seeking of dream oracles)and a "Rite of Descent" (Journey to the Tuat of Osiris, realm of the Beloved).

The concluding Chapter of the book, brings the understanding of Isis into the future and enables those accustomed to working with the Otz Chiim (Kabbalistic Tree of Life) to further cross-reference and place Isis' powers, for additional ritual applications.

Visual Keys

FIGURE # 1 : Godforms of Dynastic Egypt Located Upon the Two Lands.

FIRST KEY : Frequently Utilized Sacred Signs.

FIGURE # 2 : Annual Ritual Cycle of Ast, Queen of Sky, Earth & Tuat.

FIGURE # 3 : Daily Ritual Cycle.

SECOND KEY : Hieroglyphic Forms of Ast as Utilized in the Ancient Temples

Dedication

This work is offered with devotion to Ast and the service of Her Temple. It is with the greatest of respect that I acknowledge those who have guided me to Her altar:

Lady Olivia Robertson, Priestess Hierophant of Isis and (the late) Lord Lawrence Robertson, Priest Hierophant of Isis - both Co-Founders of The Fellowship of Isis. Influential in guiding my thinking towards Isis in a non-European way have been a trip to Africa in 1990 and the following - Iya 'l Orisa Oshun Miwa, Adupe, for showing how the Serpent dances during a workshop retreat several years ago and Baba l' Awo Fa'lokun Fatunmbi, both of the Ifa/Orisa Tradition, Adupe, for early correspondence which offered guidance on the appropriateness of all people honouring the Afrikan powers in an Afrikan way if called to do so; to Rozan, Priestess of Neith - I send love, praise and thanks for her inspirational, enduring and magickal companionship in the Mysteries and for sharing her insights into the Goddess Neith's realm. To all members of the Aset Shemsu throughout time - whose presence undoubtedly Guards and Guides the paths of all those who seek and search in Truth those past, those present and those who are to follow, this work is offered.

Life - Health - Strength.

And for Asar, the Living, loving Lord of Amen-t: Ever Youthful Remain.

4

Foreword

Never forget that ALL these people: Pharoahs and Queens, from Highest Priesthood to the least-known; all were real people once, deified now, exalted by Time passing. Yet once they, too, were flesh and blood as you are now and they, too, were my subjects, my Priesthood, my loyal and loving servants within the very same Mysteries that you now strive and seek to Understand. They, too, had to learn and they were taught and knew fully. They, the ancient and High Priesthood of a distant and powerful Time, which is here now if you persevere in My Name. They will lead you now, so listen!

Each one has a story to tell and each one who has ever called My Name and in Truth has Seen me. They will in some way assist you now to unlock the dormant Corridors and Halls of My Mysteries. For there are Passages there which have not been entered since the last footprint faded after Egypt's decline - but a new Millennium demands a renewal of power to be at hand. This has ever been an Invisible Key that in those darkest hours, when it seems that all the Greatest Lights have long-since returned, those days of chaos and despair being a Hierophantic symbol of the Adepts leaving Earth to await their return in a later time. I did not leave. I remained behind and continued to use my spells to weave new worlds for other Children to find.

What! Was it thought I vanished? She who renewed the life of Her love and brought forth the Child unaided? She who was so powerful as to get the old God's Name from His Own mouth No, I stayed and watched, mourning as My Sanctuary was left untended. I watched New Gods come and some were ME!

Hidden now and disguised in the softest garments I had ever worn. I knew, one day My Children would return to Earth, would Light the Candles would seek My aid and perhaps even ASK if I had any new plans and because I AM EVER THE UNIVERSAL MOTHER I did not turn away; So now I say See Me ! long have I awaited TO BE SEEN AS I AM : though born in the body of a woman I AM : both male and female and many other things that have been concealed to make my power less fearsome to men; have come to be preserved beneath My Seat.

"Behold, thy soul is a star living
behold! amongst its brethren." [1a]

About the cover picture

The cover picture portrays Isis in Her Solar aspect, accompanying a Queen, who is robed as Priestess of the Eygptian Temple and crowned with the Goddess' Sovereigh emblem of Upper Eygpt, the Vulture Nekhbet. The author believes this implies that the Queen, as the High Priestess, is engaged in a ceremony in which she is incarnating the Goddess as Her representative upon Earth.

Introduction

Isis is a Goddess-form familiar to not only the majority of practitioners within the Western Mystery Tradition, but also a Goddess whose fame has spread outward into the popular imagination. A clear distinction must be made and understood at the outset, between the historical ancient Egyptian Temple Traditions and the conscious creation of later times : the astral Egypt of Hermetic magick, which forms its own distinct realm, or place, upon the Inner Planes - formed from a fusion of historical Egyptian Goddess and Godforms aligned to Greek planetary principles and transposed onto the Jewish Otz Chiim (Tree of Life). That these Hermetic attributions 'work' is neither disputed nor the focus of this book and cross-references to the relevant placement upon the Tree of Life will be included to assist the modern practitioner in their work.

It is to the historical religion of the Egyptians that we turn to unveil that which has been 'lost' about Isis within the lists of correspondences - that is, Her essentially Afrikan characteristics which are understandable in the light of other Afrikan religions which have been continued in an unbroken lineage for thousands of years (remember that Egypt forms the North-East corner of the Afrikan continent). That the religion of ancient Egypt was and is a meticulous system which reveals patterns of thought and experience of the interrelationship between nature and cosmos, offering the contemporary practitioner the opportunity to work with Isis in a more ancient and perhaps, a more Traditionally Egyptian way, is the subject of this book.

Within the Egyptian religious hierarchy, Isis is not the oldest Goddess-form : before Egypt became a Dynastic Kingdom with Pharoahs and an organized Priesthood, its earliest history is as a Pre-Dynastic collection of tribes - each with its own locally revered divinities and cultus. These have always continued to exist and their worship was maintained alongside that of the Dynastic Goddesses and Gods - such as Isis - whose emergence represented a source of both religious and political power to the Pharoahs.It is because Isis' religion outlived Her Egyptian beginnings around 3,500 B.C., spreading into many parts of the world before Her 'official banishment' by the Christian Roman Emperor Theodorus in the 7th Century of our era that perhaps Her worship has been continued so strongly in modern times - for that which exists as a power can never really be 'banished' by an outsider- it merely goes into the Inner Planes until a later time when it will return.

When we refer to this majestic Goddess, using the name "Isis", many may be unaware that it is to a Greek form of this Goddess that they turn. For Isis, Osiris and Horus are all Greek renditions of their Egyptian names Ast (Isis), Asar (Osiris) and Heru (Horus) and it is within their original names that much of their power is symbolized. Some may be familiar with the Godform of Heru, but how many are aware of His mother Het-Heru (Hathor), one of the forms of Ast?

What is Ast's ancient identity? What are Her powers and formulae as constructed and worshiped in Egypt? What was the work of Her ancient Temple and priesthood and how may these be approached and utilized as a source of living power by modern minds?

Whilst acknowledging the widespread popularization of Isis as a "Lunar Goddess" forming a neat polarity with a "Solar God" consort; this was never the ancient Egyptian view - whilst Her consort / son was the Sun; the Lunar attribution was given to Gods - of learning, sciences and writing, the Patrons of Scribes, such as Lord Tehuti (Greek, Thoth) and Khons. If you work with Isis as a Lunar Goddess it is hoped that this book will bring to you a new view of her majestic, ancient powers and offer ways of approaching Her that can be utilized in addition to any well-established ritual form you may already honour. It is to the late Greek (Ptolemaic) Dynasties that Isis owes her adaptation as a Lunar goddess - in the quest to unite two countries (Egypt and Greece) with vastly different customs and religions, the priesthoods of both lands amalgamated existing divine forms, retaining only those attributions pleasing to the Greek mind-set and social customs.

It was in this amalgamation that the most potent aspects of Ast's identity were "lost", for She represented a 'difficulty' to the Greek mind, in that she was not only the source of the power of each successive Pharoah and thus a divinity of Earth as will be explained; but also a Celestial Goddess, who also had otherworldly domain in the Egyptian Tuat : "elth Isis khthonia kai Ourania". [1] There was no equivalent in the Greek Pantheon, for while they had Goddesses of the Sky (such as Hera) and Goddesses of the Otherworld (such as Persephone); they did not have a Goddess which combined all these aspects as Ast does.

The priestly 'solution' was to drop all Ast's aspects other than those which related to loving wife and mother (which She is in one aspect) and Her later ocean attribution, which had derived from sailors and travellers between the countries who navigated by Her star. It was from this stellar/ocean aspect that She eventually became known as a 'Lunar goddess' - the moon being the ruler of the sea. This 'solution' was an unfortunate one, for it divorced Ast from Her most potent aspects (particularly in the Tuat as will be revealed) in the minds of all subsequent people, but has also had negative repercussions for the role of women; both within the ancient cultures

11

and within some magical hierarchies, providing a mythic pattern to support limiting their role.

To understand who Ast is, it will be necessary to touch upon Her relationship to other Gods and Goddesses in the Egyptian system and to establish a core of iconography and symbols which specifically describe Her form and force. *It is important to understanding Ast's character to identify that She has two main forms: one BLACK and the other RED and that Her many aspects are all manifestations of these two primary forms.*

"Isis acts as the complement to the solar orientation of the scorpion Goddess, representing the night sky aspect of the feminine prototype. The solar 'red' imagery of one is countered by the Nubian 'black' imagery of the other. Isis, when encompassing both elements, is said to be born in the shape of a black and red woman." [2]

Of primary focus in this work is Ast as a Black Queen - as this is aligned to the symbolism of Her main hieroglyph the THRONE aligning Her three realms of Sky, Earth and Tuat. As a Black Queen, Ast finds a primary sphere within BINAH and this will be analysed in conjunction with the other spheres in which Her power can be recognized Kabbalistically. The Red aspect will not be dealt with in detail, as functions of this side of Her nature allude to the Innermost Mysteries of Her religion. References to this will be made symbolically, for the purpose of relatively placing the Black and Red aspects to create a unified identity and the persistent seeker may find much illumination from these forms. As She says: "I am the Nubian and have descended from heaven."[3]

Central to understanding Isis' form and force within the Egyptian system is the ideogram utilized to represent Her. "Ideograms" are hieroglyphs (Greek, 'sacred writing') which are placed either singly or in combination, depending on the name being represented, upon the head of the Goddess or God to whom they refer. This prominent usage of the head as the site of divine power is an ancient Afrikan one, heads being utilized as locus' of ancestral power and adorned and revered accordingly. This is a concept is also familiar within other traditions, such as the Crown chakra of the East and Kether upon the tree of Life. Egypt has long been spoken of as the source of much later Wisdom and whether this is to be taken literally or symbolically has been a matter of debate; it is left to the reader to decide what the undeniable similarities which exist within later religious thought could imply.

Ideograms are consonants, the Egyptian writing (like Hebrew) did not usually represent the vowels and they act as *keys* to the power of the wearer; identifying the primary forces which are embodied: they form a pictorial glyph which acts upon the transrational mind and can induce insights into the universal forces which they depict.

Once familiar with the main Ideograms used to represent the Divine realms, they can be utilised ritually in may ways (refer Chapter 2 "Transformations"). While there are several different ideograms commonly depicted upon the Goddess' head, depending upon which aspect is being referenced; Her central motif is the THRONE and in one form She is known as Ast Heru, or 'Seat of Horus' i.e. the Royal Throne (see First Key).

Being depicted as the Throne, it is clear that Ast possesses that Source of Power which enables both stability and continuity of Lineage. Ast exercises the Royal function in several ways:

1. as Divine Daughter and Sister 2. as Queen and complement of the King, Asar (Osiris) 3. as Ruler in Asar' absence when He travels abroad 4. as Queen-Mother following Asar' murder, enabling the subsequent Birth of Heru - the Child born to

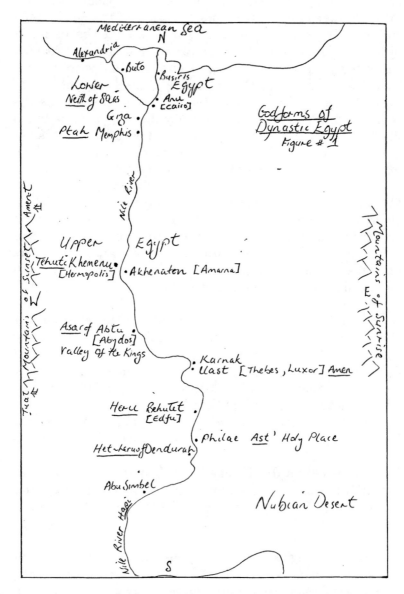

Figure # 1: Godforms of Dynastic Egypt Located Upon the Two Lands

both avenge His Father's murder and to defend His Mother against any further loss 5. as Co-Regent until Heru grew old enough to avenge this and rightly ascend the Throne 6. as Seated upon Her Throne in the Tuat (this is an aspect of Isis which has been long disacknowledged); having long-awaited the rebirth of Her Power in the form of the Daughter (Heh Final of Tetragrammaton - see the concluding Chapter "Power of the Ages..").

While "Nature furnishes the earliest gods - the national state makes early impression on religion - its forms pass over into the world of the gods - their origin and function in nature retire into the background - the gods become active in the sphere of human affairs" [(4)]. On one level the gods become political archetypes, which both set the patterns for the way the earthly Kings and Queens rule and are viewed, but also conversely, the gods themselves begin to be molded in the same manner; their representations, forms and functions mirroring that of the Pharoah.

This is very true of Ast and also of many other Dynastic Gods and Goddesses. That Ast's connection to the Throne could be and was utilized in legitimising earthly rulers is an historical fact. Each successive Pharoah - of which Ast was the Divine Ancestress - was only fully empowered by being 'seated in the Goddess lap '- i.e. literally Enthroned, but also an allusion to the symbolic 'Enthronement' which was enacted in the form of a 'Divine Marriage' between the Pharoah and the Highest Priestess of Ast (Her Earthly incarnation) an office ever filled by His own Eldest Sister. The symbolic act of suckling was also a key to His power; this was a legal form of adoption in ancient Egypt and explains why so many statues exist of the Pharoah, in the position of Child-Heru at Ast's breast; the public positioning of such statues reinforced that Pharoah was both Divine and Son of the Goddess; but on another level this also acknowledged that She was the Source of the Power of 'His' Throne.

1.

Isis, Queen of the World

The first key to understanding Ast is that of Sovereignty. As will be seen, She was clearly and repeatedly addressed, in Her own Temples and by Her priesthood as Queen of three realms - Sky (Above, the Stellar regions, the East); Earth (Upper Egypt, the South and after Unification also Lower Egypt, the North); and Tuat (Below, the Ancestral regions, the West); the title of this chapter being a praise name from one of the Hymns inscribed upon the wall of Ast's primary Temple at Philae (for full discussion see Chapter "ur heka" - which includes Hymns of Praise and and other Words of Power).

Her Queenship derived from a Divine hereditary lineage; Ast being the eldest daughter of the union of the Sky Goddess Nut (Nu, Nuit) and the Earth God Geb (Keb), these being two of the Ennead - Nine Divinities descended from Ra-Atum representing aspects of creation (Shu,Tefnet, Geb, Nut, Asar, Heru, Set, Ast, Neb-t het). From Her mother, She inherited sovereignty of the Sky and from Her father, the Throne of the Earth; through the marriage to Her brother Asar (Osiris), the eldest son, the rulership of Egypt was doubly reinforced. On the one hand, these are representations of the actual inter-marriages between brother and sister which occurred within the Egyptian royal family, to ensure the 'purity' of the blood royal. On the other hand, the marriage of these two divinities represents the dynamic union of opposite elemental principles and the ensuing balance and fecundity which results.

Examining the primary hieroglyphic forms of Ast (see Hieroglyphic Forms of Ast List in Chapter 7 - "Annual Cycles of Renewal".) - reveals that She was equally a Goddess-form of Above and Below; consistent with that of Her consort Asar, who likewise ruled in the land of Mer (Egypt) and later in the otherworldly realm of the Tuat as Seker ("Silence"). In keeping with the Egyptian view of the sky realms, Ast, like all Goddesses and Gods, Ast was seen to be the manifestation of a particular star; Her stellar aspect being Ast Septit (Sep-t = Greek: Sothis, Sirius).

Ast's manifestations in the realms of Sky, Earth and Tuat form a complementary power to Asar's manifestations in the realms of Sun, Nile and Tuat. She was both the sky wherein the sun was daily reborn and the tears (rain) which caused the Nile (Asar) to flood, fecundating the land. In keeping with Egyptian notions of duality and androgyny, Asar was both the Nile (all Gods were seen to be manifestations of the androgynous Nile God Hapi /Hepr, as the Nile was the source of life) and the corn which grew from the fecundated Land; the Land itself being seen as Ast.

It is important, in order to assimilate the elemental shifts which occur within the ancient manifestations of these Great Ones, to realise that the Egyptian view was not an either/or one; it was a multiple and encompassing "many-valued logic" (5), which employed a symbolic code, deriving from male and female sexual functions. These functions were presented as emanating from both Goddesses and Gods - as complementary and not mutually exclusive forces. The high number of self-creative/parthenogenic divine forms within the Egyptian system (e.g. Atum, Khephra, Neit, Hapi, Ast in Tuat etc.) were the means by which the priesthood were able to resolve existential issues relating to the Life-Death /Space-Time continuum; the amorphous presentation of the divine realm being meant as a trigger to unlock the divine powers of Creation within human potential.

Within the legends and tales of the divine lives, the imagery of male and female interacting and exchanging roles, is another manifestation of androgyny; which "is an archaic and universal formula for the expression of wholeness, the coexistence of the contraries, or the coincidentia oppositorum.. symbolizes the perfection of a primordial, non-conditioned state."(6) It is my view that Ast exemplifies this state; the hieroglyphic forms by which She was worshiped and the attendant animal symbolism (see Chapter "Transform-ations" for ritual applications) provides an ancient perspective of wholeness/unity - the attaining of which is surely one of the primary goals of all magickal/spiritual endeavour - and one which is equally inspirational for both women and men to follow today.

Ast as the principle of Sovereignty represents a central point of power within the Egyptian system. "The role of the Throne (st) as the maker (ir) of the King is well known for punning on the throne and eye in the name of Osiris"; which is wst ir ("Seat of the Eye")/wsir/Asar in hieroglyphics. Both "Throne" and "Eye" are particular elemental forces inherited by their children (see final Chapter).

As to how Ast became known as Isis: "phonetic laws which produced the Coptic NHCE from the ancient Egyptian nst "Throne" were responsible for the evolution of the ancient Egyptian st "throne","seat" to HCE the Coptic form of the name Isis."(7) Through analysis of the hieroglyph used as the ideogram of Her name and the consonants that make up that name - ST - it is clear that both 'Ast' and 'Isis' are the equivalents of our English word 'Throne'. Take some time to reflect on what this means - how does it alter your perception of who this Goddess is?

The force which is embodied within the form of Ast = Sovereign Authority; however there is nothing of the tyrant or the cruel ruler here. As Queen, She was much loved by the people of Egypt,ruling in Asar' absence when He travelled abroad, teaching agriculture and growing the first corn (both literal and symbolic of bringing forth the Sun). She was also keenly aware of the need to maintain stability in the Land through a legitimate heir to the Throne being produced and after Asar' unjust murder by His younger brother, who sought to usurp the Throne, She overcame Her great sorrows to achieve this goal. Searching endlessly for Him, flooding the Land with tears,with great love and with the assistance of Lord Tehuti (Greek, Thoth) and Lord Anpu (Greek, Anubis); Asar' dismembered body was found, reconstituted (the first act of embalming) and installed as King in the Tuat, where Ast journeyed to in the company of her adoptive son Anpu, the "Opener of the Ways". There in the depths of the Tuat, in solitary, She performed Her greatest act of magick - in one manifestation of Her Red aspect - She resurrected the Godhead of Asar, to enable regeneration of His essence.

It is because the nature of Ast's power is a balanced force, that She embodies the prerequisite composition for generation; the Throne being a 'masculine' hieroglyph; whilst the 'Eye' ( ) can be interpreted as ' feminine '; in addition to its symbolic usage as a solar /sexual glyph. It is this allusion to a magickal androgyny, suggestive of an inversion of roles between Ast and Asar (i.e He is dead/dismembered, She is living and recreates what is 'lost') that forms another potent example of the way Egyptian religious thought maintained the original unity of the creator (itm/Atum) - who was Himself a self-creative androgyne force. This "unity" represents the summit of attainment. the Sovereign Divine force, the Kether of the Tree of Life. The relative positions of Ast and Asar in this part of the legends can be likened to the relative roles of Kali/Shiva within the Hindu system; whilst acknowledging cultural particularities and certain differences of intention.

It is also interesting to note that the consonant " t " is used as an ending to Goddess' names, such as As-t; Nebt-het (Greek,

Nepthys); Nei-t; Neb-t-seker (the Necropolis Cobra goddess complement to He-t-heru (Greek, Hathor) i.e. the Death-Birth axis); Sekhme-t etc; as well as for the word denoting a "Lady" (Neb-t). This consonant "t" is used as both a female determinative hieroglyph (Egyptian, like many languages, is 'gendered') and as an ancient letter denoting the SCARAB. In one way, its usage as an ending to goddess-names is a symbolic means of creating a balanced force within these Goddesses. The "t" then becomes both a' feminine' and a ' masculine' consonant, an example of an androgynous magickal letter. It is interesting to note that the Scarab was widely used/carried as a protective symbol. The Scarab, "t", also represents the animal form in which Khephra - one of the primordial, self-creative god-forms, incarnates. This suggests that the usage of this letter 'concealed a scarab aspect' that exists within the Goddesses and symbolises a potent primal creative/birth potential, that far exceeds the' birth' power that we have experience of as humans. This also expresses the fullness of power that women were accorded within the Egyptian mysteries and to which they can aspire magickally today.

The role of Isis as Queen and the role of Her representative, the wife of Pharoah and the highest priestess, combined the functions related to several important areas: that of her relationship to the King and the responsibilities of leading the Royal cult activities; which required the full spectrum of female aspects to be embodied: sister /daughter and wife / mother /. Several women were required to fill these roles, thus the household of Pharoah contained a number women (his sisters), all 'Queens', presided over by the highest in rank (first marriage, the eldest).

This, in turn, is both a reflection of and reflected in the divine realm; Ast's twin sister Neb-t het (Greek, Nepthys), being an embodiment of the complementary principles; She was dusk (or the hours of darkness/portion of the sky preceding dawn);

whilst Ast was the dawn (both the hours of the Solar Disc arising and that portion of the sky where the rising occurred). Both Goddesses have an intimate relationship with their eldest brother Asar; from the union of Asar and Neb-t het (unbeknownst to Ast'), Anpu (Greek, Anubis) is born.

It may come as a surprise to readers familiar with the Egyptian hierarchy to realise that it is Anubis who is the firstborn son of Osiris and not Heru (Heru was not engendered upon Ast until after Asar' murder, see "Transformations"). The reason that the royal line is reckoned through Heru, is because Ast was the eldest daughter, the traditional heir of the royal power and the legitimate wife.It is because of the inheritance being passed through the eldest daughter that the intermarriage of brother to sister was necessary for the brother to ascend the throne. Understanding these intrigues helps to explain the later actions of Ast in relation to Anpu, whom She adopts and then maintains as Her closest companion and Guide.

The presence of Two Sons of Osiris, is fully in keeping with the duality inherent in all Egyptian religious thought; the Throne of Isis itself having a double nature. The "st" Throne has an alignment with the power of Asar, being a component of His Name as has been previously explained. The 'other' Throne is that of Ast's royal twin sister, Neb-t het which was spelt originally as Nbt-Hwt; the "het / hwt" part of the name is the "house" or "temple" which forms the enclosure wherein the Sun is nurtured and born; Ast in Her form of Het-heru (Greek, Hathor). In this manner, one Throne is specifically aligned to Heru and alludes to the double nature of the Egyptian Kingship; a duality represented in a variety of religious and secular motifs, such as the Two Feathers; Two Eyes; Two Lands(Upper and Lower Egypt);Two Ladies; Two Cobras; Two Horizons etc.

That Two Thrones were always present and occupied by different gods is supported by numerous stelae and inscriptions. Of particular interest is the seating of Heru (Horus) upon one throne and the seating of Anpu (Anubis) upon the other. This leads to the hypothesis that parallel and complementary times exist (see final Chapter). The presence of a chthonic ruler in harmony with Horus, also goes along way to ridding this archetypal cycle of the ages old Horus/Set antagonism/conflict; which had a validity and need a long time ago and which, once achieved of its goal, really needed to be re-evaluated/updated in the light of current and future developments. That ' mythic cycles' such as these are not 'set in stone' - but continue to live and develop, having a 'life' of their own - would be apparent to any practitioners who have engaged in devoted work with them; the inability, or unwillingness, to assimilate current developments in such a cycle, is perhaps due to the use of the powers in support of a pre-determined result,which relies upon maintaining fixed narratives. Like the ancient Egyptian priesthood, it is necessary to maintain the dynamism within the divine realms; this can only be achieved by a continuous creation and the ability of modern devotees/priestesses and priests to be willing to translate it.

The seating of Her two Sons upon these Two Thrones, has the potential to enable the meticulous patterns inherent within the ancient Egyptian religious thought to begin to become understood as a living reality. Lord Anpu, the constant companion and Guide of Ast is connected to both Her stellar birthplace (Above) Sep-t (Greek, Sothis/Sirius); the Land of Egypt (Necropolis) and the Tuat (Below). Lord Heru, the avenger and protector, is connected to the Sky realm and the North Pole constellations of Bootes, Orion and Ursa Major - His traditional stellar birthplace (Above) (8); the Land of Egypt and also has a Tuat aspect (Below). That each Son rules predominately in one or the other realm, does not prevent them having power in the other realms; in keeping with the

Divine ability to go and to go forth by day and by night. If we posit Heru as an 'Above' god-form due to Him being a Hawk and if we position Anpu as a 'Below ' god-from, due to His ability to 'Open the Ways' between worlds, we must not forget their ability/power in the other realms.

Sep-t, the 'Dogstar' has as its hieroglyph a five-pointed star; compare this to the symbol for the Egyptian chthonic realm, the Tuat (this same star encircled). The harmonious nature of these parallel Thrones will be beginning to become apparent, as will the forces which their Mother, Ast embodies. They represent the dual acts of ascension and descension; anabolism and catabolism; both Outer Space and Inner Space; Past, Present and Future forming a continuum of time which meets at, and can be accessed at, the horizon through the Hidden Gate of which Lord Anpu is the sole Gatekeeper. Each realm can be viewed as both a separate place, that can be visited through Ritual Journeys and a state of mind - that can be accessed within the individual practitioner (see Chapters Rite of Ascent and Rite of Descent).

2.

Transformations

An important feature of Egyptian religious thought and practise is the recognition of the divine principle and its manifestation in anthropomorphic (animal/human) form and the representation of these principles within ritual objects. Based upon an inspired, detailed observation of the lifestyle and habitats of the animals native to the local environment; different aspects of the neter were represented as manifesting in particular animals. In Pre-Dynastic Egypt, these animals were solely revered as the embodiment of the divine and as the Clan ancestor. As time passed and with the establishment of the Dynastic head (Pharoah) as the primary external focus of power; the Priesthood were inspired to construct composite forms which combined the forms of the ancient animal realms with the human realm. Eventually the divine was presented in human form, with an animal headdress only. These serve as both pictorial representations of the name of the wearer (see Ideogram discussion previous) and as potent glyphs of the power of the elemental and cosmic forces which they represent. The presentation of the neter in composite form is a means to focus the mind, reminding it that it is an abstract principle that is being honoured or Invoked.

Ast has several potent animal transformations in which aspects of Her power are manifested, revealing a form approachable and recognizable to the human mind. Objects which are imbued with these forces, in the form s of a part of animal or plant sacred to Ast, also have important functions within ritual performance and the Temple service. In this regard there were Guilds of skilled artisans in the service of each Temple to furnish such requirements - this is an area where any artistic skills we may possess may come into full use in a sacred context.

The ancients created rituals and legends to elaborate existing things - such as objects commonly in use and found within these a harmony with both celestial and terrestrial phenomena. Objects and furnishings associated with the day-to-day life of Pharoah's Household were also ritualised and form an important place in Ast's Temple; an example of this being the Throne: a literal Coronation Seat, a symbol of Sovereign power and a representation of this employed in rituals when Pharoah was absent. Many exquisitely carved and gilded examples of this type of Throne have been removed from amongst the Funerary Treasures buried with the royal families.

It was customary to have the symbol for the Unification of the Two Lands - the Lotus and Papyrus tied together surrounding the same emblem; this ever reminded of the great power which the Throne both possessed and carried. It is important to note, that as the Highest Priest, Pharoah would have been well aware that this Throne was a physical representation of Ast, His Goddess and Queen, in whose lap he sat and by right of blood relation to Her, did he reign. An object of absolute pre-eminence, the Throne as ritual object is aligned to Ast in the Elder- Mother form of the Vulture, Nekhbet - the foundation of the power of Upper Egypt; this finds a natural placement upon the Tree of Life manifesting within the Saturnian Sphere of Binah and a the Throne of Earth, within Malkuth.

Particular features of animals, such as their horns or wings, were also utilised as ritual objects to denote the strength of the whole animal. A widely recognized example of this, is perhaps Ast in Her most popular form of the Solar Het-heru; the use of golden horns and solar disc denote fecundity and generative strength, the power of the divine Mother, who in one form Mehurit is the celestial cow whose four legs represent each of the four compass points of Earth. Sphere: Tiphareth and Netzach.

The Papyrus, the sacred plant emblem of Lower Egypt and the emblem of Scribes, provides another example of the usage of one thing to denote much more. When placed side by side, roots tied together, Lotus and Papyrus formed the gesture called sam taui and represented the Union of the Two Lands. Lotus is attributed to Sphere: Binah and Yesod; Papyrus to: Binah and Hod. Both Lotus and Papyrus may be represented in a permanent form of sceptre or wand (as anciently).

In this connection, the use of the sceptre, or wand, finds itself represented amongst the three important ritual objects utilised to invoke Life-Health-Strength; or Ankh-Tjed-Uas. These three blessings were bestowed upon all important individuals, either before or after their names and also feature as engravings upon the portal entrances to both temples and regions of the Tuat (see chapter 10 - Rite of Descent). As individual sacred objects, the Ankh is also held by divinities and denotes their power of both bestowing and maintaining life; but also the Ankh is used as a sign to invoke their ability 'to go', or to move between worlds unhindered. In shape the Ankh represents the union of the male and female principles in a harmonious whole and though often inter-preted only as a sexual glyph, it can also be viewed as an androgynous sign - as it contains both principles combined so as to form a third and new form. In this manner the Ankh is indeed a 'key', as it is so often called; for it reaffirms the underlying patterns inherent within all Egyptian religious thought - that of the power of the original creator Atum (itm) who was 'himself' an androgyne god-form - and it is within this androgyny that the most potent aspects of life are called into being and expressed. No matter which gender you are physically housed in, to work with these ancient principles, the power of Ankh must be embraced and invoked, with the ultimate goal of experiencing union within yourself; that is uniting the two principles and enabling them to be fully illumined within. Sphere: Tiphareth.

The second of these principles, Tjed, is symbolised by the ritual object which is a pillar with a tall base leading to four sections; this is often said to be either the vertebrae and spinal column of Ast's beloved Asar (Osiris), a stylisation of His organs of fecundity, or a representation of the sacred palm tree. To work with this principle invokes physical health and longevity; in this regard all three of the above interpretations of the glyph are in harmony and so may be utilised interchangeably to add depth of understanding to the sign. The palm tree in particular adds great blessing to the underlying meaning of the Tjed-sign; for it is the Egyptian Tree of Life and of similar importance to the Jewish Otz Chiim. The palm is utilised within Ast's Temple also in other connections, particularly to represent the victory which is achieved by reaching certain thresholds of power and successfully entering across them. Sphere: Tiphareth and Netzach.

The Uas sceptre completes these three blessings and invokes the power of peaceful authority: a strength independent of violence,menace,treachery and bloodshed. As such, it should be viewed with great reverence, for the wielding of Uas invokes such authority within the astral ambience of the user and is a power that should not be abused or violated by using it for aggressive or tyrannical purposes. That the power of peaceful strength is neither weak, nor passive; but promotes an environment where much can be attained without opposition and that this should be a highly desirable state for magickal practitioners is apparent (for further discussion of

Ast's wielding of Uas, see chapter 4 "Ur Heka"). Sphere: Chokmah.

Aligned in similar symbolism to the Tjed - pillar and often represented at its side in inscriptions as a means of denoting the brother/sister, god/goddess pair of Asar and Ast, is Ast's Tet sign; this may be ritually symbolised by a sacred red cord, worn around the waist and looped so as to form a figure of eight-like buckle shape. Alternatively, a red ribbon or other red thread may be placed upon the altar to denote Tet. This sign invokes protection upon the wearer and in ancient times was also carved into red glass and red jasper. That it represents the feminine organs of the Goddess and their natural functions becomes apparent through meditation, as may other uses for this ritual object, its living counterparts and the mysteries of the interrelated Sa sign.

This most sacred of ritual signs is frequently encountered when working with Red aspects of the Goddess and related forms. In this connection, a ritual object in the form of a Boat-shaped vessel of golden metal with a serpent handle may also be created and utilised symbolically. Sphere: Geburah, Netzach,Yesod.

A further ritual object expressing these mysteries is the Menat; this sign combined representations of two vessels in conjunction and was always worn at the end of a long collar by both the goddess in Her forms of Het-heru and Mehurit and by priestesses of this aspect. The Menat is distinguished with the ability to restore the reproductive powers in the Tuat and is also associated with fertility, attraction of opposites and fecundity in this life.

As has been noted, the reproductive powers as condensed within the symbolic representation of the ankh allude to the most potent of powers and also the ability to move without hindrance between worlds. It is the connection of the ability to

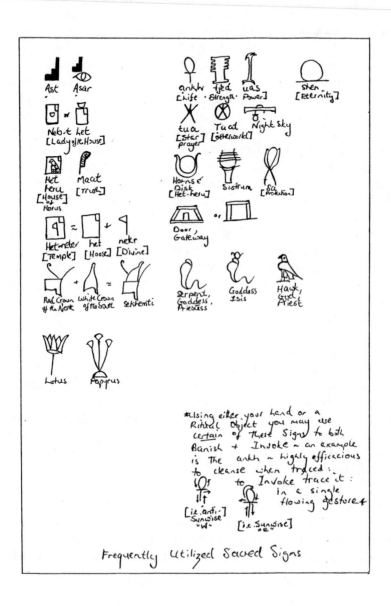

Ast Asar

ankh [Life] tjed [Strength] uas [Power] shen [Eternity]

Nebt het [Lady of the House]

tua [Star prayer] Tuat [Otherworld] Night Sky

Het heru [House of Horus] Maat [Truth]

Horns & Disk [Het-heru] Sistrum Sa [Protection]

Het-neter [Temple] het [House] nekr [Divine]

Door, Gateway

Red Crown of the North White Crown of the South Sekhemti

Serpent, Goddess, Priestess Goddess Isis Hawk, God, Priest

Lotus Papyrus

*Using either your hand or a Ritual Object you may use certain of these Signs to both Banish + Invoke ~ an example is The ankh ~ highly efficacious to cleanse when traced:
to Invoke trace it in a single flowing gesture*
[i.e. anti-Sunwise "W"] [i.e. Sunwise "E"]

Frequently Utilized Sacred Signs

transform oneself at will, both in this life and the afterlife and the interconnecting powers of mobility and fertility that offer a series of keys into the deepest mind of the ancient Egyptian priesthood and the profound reverence for life essential to the modern magician and appreciation for the great gift of freedom, which enables the work. There is also mapped out the means of movement between worlds and lives; in the cycle of transformations from Tuat reborn via the womb. In this cycle the powers symbolised within the ankh-tjed-tet-menat ritual objects are the focus.

Returning to the solar glory of Ast, another object frequently encountered in ritual is the mirror; particularly in connection with the worship of Het-heru, the Mother of the Sun daily reborn from Amen-t and symbolised as the solar disc being raised from between Her regal horns. Whilst horns were held in reverence amongst many cultures anciently and featured within the Temple as symbols of both the female cow and male bull, being representative of the Mother and Her Son-Lover; it is the mirror which serves solely as a glyph of female solar power.

In the Egyptian language, one of the words used to represent a 'mirror' was also the same as that used to denote 'life'; that is ankh. It is because of the connection the mirror has with the sense of sight and the act of seeing and also the necessity of light to this, that the mirror was associated with protection and the ability to deter, or reflect away negativity. In addition to being related to the beneficent qualities of light and life associated with Tiphareth; the role of the mirror was also denoted by several distinct words apart from ankh: ir; un her and mau-her ( ). These variations suggest different kinds of mirrors; or that there were specific mirrors utilised for both sacred and secular use.

Due to the profound holiness of the word ankh, it is most likely that the ankh- mirror was the one denoted for use in ritual as a whole object and also for amulet use. Mirrors of this type decorated lavishly have been located amongst the funerary offerings of the Pharoahs. Sphere: also Yesod.

In connection with creating the appropriate ambience within the Temple, the musical instrument called the sistrum is carried by priestesses. This sacred object is shaped in the form of an ankh-sign, with four wires strung across the loop which hold disks. These four represent the elemental powers which are called into operation within ritual and the shaking of the sistrum is utilised to banish negativity and bring joy to the worship. Sphere: Netzach.

A final important ritual object in the worship of Ast is the Lamp; its bright light representing the perpetual aspiration and inner sanctuary of the devotee. At certain times within the annual ritual cycle, the use of lamps or lights, becomes the focus of the work. An example of this is the June 24 ceremony called "The Lighting Of The Lamps" (see Chapter 6) which was performed simultaneously within both Ast's Temple at Philae and Neith's Temple at Sais. This solemn processional and illumination of these temples annually represented the Unification of Upper and Lower Egypt. Connected to Ast, particularly in Her Stellar aspect, the lamp is a ritual object which is both easy to obtain and beautiful to behold. In this regard it is interesting to note that the hieroglyph for 'star' is in the form of a lamp hanging from the vault of the sky. Sphere: Daath.

ANIMAL	NAME	ASPECT
VULTURE	Nekhbet NeterMut	Sovereign emblem of Upper Egypt;White Crown;Lotus Sceptre; "st" Throne; Divine Mother Ast ur-t mut neter; Necropolis guardian and

		Nursing Mother of the Dead. Manifests in Binah, Malkuth.
COBRA	Uadjet Iaret Ur-aeus Neb-t seker Necropolis	Sovereign emblem of Lower Egypt; Red Crown; Papyrus Sceptre; Divine Daughter; Neb-t aakhu; Ast uraeus; guardian. Manifests: Binah, Geburah, Tiphareth.

*A Serpent hieroglyph was used generically to represent the words "Goddess; Priestess; Woman" in this same manner, a Hawk was used to represent "God; Priest; Man".

KITE & SWALLOW		Tuat forms to enable Birth of Heru.
COW	Het-heru Me-hurit	Mother of the Dawn Sun. The Celestial Cow who supports the sky and whose four legs represent N, S, E, W. Patroness of birth, fecundity, joy.Manifests:Tiphareth, Netzach.
GOOSE	Negg-ur Gengen-ur	A form of Het-heru; The great goose God/dess whose egg represents the reborn sun of dawn. The 'ur' part of the name refers to this 'great' act/ moment of 'rising'.
SCORPION	Selket Serket Tabityt	Ast ta-uh; Red Queen. Manifests: Geburah.

HIPPOPOT AMUS	Taur-t Ast	Majestic Nile Goddess of birth; the central godform of the Denderah Zodiac.
LION	Sekhmet	The warrior aspect of Het-heru; Ast-Rait-set; one of forms of the solar Eye. Manifests: Tiphareth, Geburah.
CAT	Bast	Ba-en-ast; Ast's Ba; Patron and protector of home and family; psychic protection; giver of joy; the domesticated, benign form of Sekhmet. Manifests: Netzach, Yesod.

Within ritual, these sacred objects are utilised both to invoke the powers they hold as described and also as representatives of Ast Herself. If the physical object is not available, another way of working with these forms is through tracing the sign in the air before you, either with your dominant hand, or whilst holding a wand or sceptre. In these instances it is usual to begin tracing the sign from the bottom left-hand corner in a sunwise (clockwise) direction to invoke the power and beginning in the bottom right-hand corner and tracing in an anti-clockwise direction to use the sign to banish, or remove unwanted atmosphere/cleanse your ritual area. It is important to keep firmly in mind the meaning of each of the Egyptian signs if you intend to use them either to banish or invoke, for they hold specific forces and are not able to be used in the generic manner that a practitioner accustomed to using either the pentagram (microcosm/elemental/earth sign) or a hexagram (macrocosm/ planetary/solar sign) applies these signs.

As to the transformations of the Goddess into animal forms, as the accompanying list reveals; Ast was a multi-faceted Goddess whose powers could not be contained or represented by one animal form alone. Each of the animals revered describes a particular aspect of Her vast force and may also be applied to one of the realms of Earth,Sky, or Tuat in particular. Here follows the Days of the Week most suitable to the work with each of these animal-forms:

MONDAY: Ba-en -Ast (Bast); Patroness/Protectress of
              Home, family, psychic; Cat; Yesod.
TUESDAY: Red Queen; Scorpion; Selket;Serquet;
              Geburah.
WEDNESDAY: Ast, Mistress of Magick, She who possesses
              the ur heka; Hod.
THURSDAY: Ast-Maat, the Throne of Truth in the
              Kingdom of Asar; Kite; Swallow; Chesed.
FRIDAY: Het-heru as pleasure principle; Cow;
              Hippopotamus; Netzach.
SATURDAY: Ast as Vulture Queen Nekhbet; Binah.
SUNDAY: Het-heru; Mehurit; Negg-ur; Sekhmet; Cow;
              Goose; Lioness; Cobra; Tiphareth.

The animal transformations re-affirm the interrelationship of the three realms, with reference in particular to one or the other place; whilst the sovereign emblems of Vulture and Cobra have dominion which spans and unifies all three realms:

EARTH	**SKY**	**TUAT**
Cobra	Vulture	Vulture
Cow.........also...........	(Solar)	Cobra
Goose.......also..........	(Solar)	Kite
Lioness.....also...........	(Solar)	Swallow
Cat...........also...........	(Solar/Lunar)	
Hippopotamus..also..	(Stellar)	
Scorpion		

In addition to the various animal transformations being representative of these realms; the interrelationship of the animal forms to each other must also be kept n mind. An example of this interplay is found within the solar aspects of Het-heru (Cow /Horns and Disk motif) a beneficent aspect who transforms into -Sekhmet (Lioness) a warrior and destructive aspect who then transforms into the gentle feline Bast, a Protectress. Another example are the Cow and Hippopotamus, who both fulfil a solar birthing role and the Cow and Goose, which also embody this aspect. Close meditation upon these various incarnations of the Goddess also reveals that the primary functions which the embodiment of her forces perform, can be summarised under the areas of 1. Sovereignty and maintenance of the royal lineage 2. Rebirthing of the solar principle 3. Defence and protection 4. Regeneration and fecundity 5. Patroness of magick.

In addition to manifesting within the three realms of Earth, Sky and Tuat, as noted; the animal forms of Ast find a natural alignment with the three seasons of the Egyptian calendar: Earth -Winter Proye; Sky - Summer Shomu; Tuat - Inundation Akhe (see chapter. 9 for fuller discussion). Looking closely at the animal forms of the Earth realm, it becomes apparent that these also manifest within the sky realm - the difference is not in aspect, but in the intensity of the force projected.In one sense,when manifesting within the realm of Earth the force is in an introvert form; when manifesting within the realm of Sky, the force assumes an extrovert form.

Another way of understanding the applications of these forces is through astrological alignment:

SIGN	GODDESS	ANIMAL FORM
Aquarius	Nut	Woman
Pisces	Taur-t	Hippopotamus
Aries	Tabity; Sekhmet	Falcon; Lioness
Taurus	Het-heru; Mehurit	Cow
Gemini	Ast/Neb-t-het; Nekhbet; Uadjit	Woman; Vulture; Cobra
Cancer	Bast	Cat
Leo	Sekhmet; Bast	Lioness; Cat
Virgo	Ast	Woman
Libra	Ast-Maat	Woman; Ostrich
Scorpio	Selket; Serquet	Scorpion
Sagittarius	Neith	Cobra
Capricorn	Nekhbet; Uadjit	Vulture; Cobra

God-forms traditionally aligned to certain of the astrological signs such as: Amun, Ra, Heru (Aries); Khonsu (Cancer); Thoth (Libra &Virgo); Asar (Capricorn); Hapi (Pisces); may also be usefully employed in conjunction with the goddess-forms.

A further application of the divine animal transformations within ritual work is through alignment to the four quadrants, in an Egyptian form of the Hebrew Chaia ha Qadesh - the four Holy Living Creatures or Kerubs. Practitioners unfamiliar with them in this form may be more familiar with them as the Kerubs of the fixed zodiacal signs: to Aquarius, the Man and East; to Taurus, the Bull and North; to Leo the Lion and South; to Scorpio the Eagle and West. These four Holy Living Creatures may be utilised as stations in their respective elemental corners. An Egyptian version of this places the Hawk (East); Vulture (South); Jackal (West); Cobra (North). In this format, the Sovereign emblems of Upper and Lower Egypt find their natural placement at the South and North and also represent the principle of the Mother-Daughter; whilst the East-West axis is empowered by the Father-Son principle as represented within the reborn Hawk of Dawn and the Jackal of the Tuat.

Further to this is natural alignment of goddess and god-forms to the elemental quarters and to the Kerubs: Goddess-forms: Ast (East); Het-heru (South); Neb-t-het (West); Neb-t-seker (North). God-forms: Heru (East); Anpu (South); Asar (West);Tehuti (North).

In another pattern, Lord Anpu may be ascribed to Below as a Guiding and Guardian God-form, particularly in Rites of Descent; whilst Lord Tehuti may be ascribed to Above as a source of outpouring Divine Wisdom.

Within these particular sequences of Goddess-forms, Ast finds Her complement within the Western quadrant and Her dark twin sister Neb-t-het (Nepthys); similarly Het-heru (Hathor) a Goddess of solar birth, finds the complementary power within the Northern quadrant and the necropolis Guardian Neb-t seker (also known as Mert-seger; Her name translates as Neb-t=Lady+ seker=silence; particularly fitting for a Goddess of the Death aspect).

Likewise with the God-forms; the solar Hawk of Dawn, Heru, finds His complementary power within the Western region and His Father, Asar, whose re-incarnation Heru represents; whilst Jackal headed Anpu, the constant Companion of Ast, Guards the region of His adoptive mother, the South; with Lord Tehuti (Wisdom) giving guidance to the North. It is fitting that these two God-forms flank the Father-Son axis, as Anpu is the first-born of Asar, as has been discussed and Tehuti represents the patron Magician-God whose Wisdom unites above and below and by whom Ast was guided to enable her to perform the great act of love which enabled Asar to be reborn in the form of Heru.

When invoked into a prepared and purified ritual sphere, the practitioner may either 1.Visualise the respective goddess or god as incarnate within their animal transformation; 2. Visualise their ideogram infused with the eternally pure light of creation and projected to the respective cardinal direction; 3. Envision yourself in either the animal form with the ideogram atop your head, or in the human - form these powers assume with the particular ideogram atop your head. This last technique of assuming the form of the goddess or god requires utmost attention to detail within the mind of the practitioner and is best not attempted until a full and thorough familiarity with the forms of the powers is gained and until these details can be recalled easily and clearly, at will. With all work of this nature, it is also assumed that the deepest sincerity, love and devotion to the gods, in accordance with the aspiration of fulfilment of the practitioner's highest good aim and pure, true will, is the underlying motivation.

Despite the numerous manifestations discussed, the power of the goddess-form is always available within the condensed form of the ideogram and also within the headdress. Examples of how the headdress may be utilised as an identifier of power are: Horns and Disc = Solar Mother (East, South); Throne = Sovereign Queen (May be used in all directions, depending upon purpose); Vulture = Queen/Mother (South); Cobra = Princess/Daughter (North); Throne and Feather = Mother and Daughter (East-West /North-South). Combinations of these forms indicate an all-embracing form of Ast. As suggested above, these headdresses may also be employed in the form of a glyph, tracing the pattern in the air before you - at the appropriate quadrant - as you infuse it with the pure Light of Creation.

The Animal Forms of Isis
Cat: a well-known Goddess is the Cat or Cat-headed Bast. What is usually not recognized about Bast, is that She

represents the Ba-en-Ast, or the eternal and pure heart-soul of Ast which enabled Her form to live within the Tuat. The name 'Bast' is a compression of Her full name into one word. A hint of its otherworldly and Western aspect is provided by the Black-Cat form of statues which Bast is usually depicted in. The Black giving reference to both the ancestral regions, the sphere of night and the Saturnian time with which the journey through eternity is made. It is because of the re-animating and eternally protective role that the 'Cat', or Ba, plays within the lore of Ast, that by extension, She became revered as a protector of the place of dwelling and also the psychic sphere. Seek Bast's blessing upon your home and family and also upon night-time journeys-both those undertaken in the wider world and those undertaken on the inner planes and through the ancestral regions.

Cow: one of the most widely known forms is Ast in Her transformation as the Celestial Cow Mehurit, an earlier form of the cow Het-heru. In this aspect, Ast is responsible for the daily rebirth of the solar disc from its night-time abode and journey through the Tuat, or the region of Amen-t. It is this animal-form which is referred to when you see depictions of the Goddess with either a cow's head, or crowned with the Horns and Disc headdress. The cow form represents a benevolent and joyous Goddess, whose Temples were renowned for their feasting, drinking and fecund rites. Work with this aspect for 'green' rites dedicated to fecundity, fertility, love, abundance, health, environmental welfare, Earth-rites, creativity, pregnancy, birth, solar consciousness and the power to bring forth that which you conceive (this can equally apply to works of art, writing and other endeavours as much as it can to, literal childbirth).

Kite: in this lesser-known form of small hawk, Ast makes Her descent into the Western region of the Tuat and there unites with Her beloved Asar and becomes pregnant with the child-hawk, Heru. Transforming into this small hawk was vitally necessary to enable Ast to be able to bring forth her son in the form of a hawk, through the principle of like bringing forth like. Within the Egyptian system, birds are considered to have the 'power to go' - the power of free movement between worlds and so are particularly suited to both above and below works.

This Hawk-form of Ast was annually celebrated within Her Temple of Denderah, where a sacred Hawk lived and was revered as an incarnation of the Goddess. Within the related Temple of Heru at Edfu, a similar Hawk dwelled and was revered as an incarnation of the God. Once each year the Hawk at Edfu made the long journey to Denderah, where the Hawks were mated in a rite of high religious and secular importance.This in all ways parallels the lore of Ast's work in the Tuat and it is essential to working with this form of Ast, to understand both the central importance of this transformation and the subsequent responsibilities. It is not appropriate to use this form for any works except those which are of the highest and which unite both principles in such a manner as will enable the regeneration of the Temple.

Hippopotamus: this majestic animal finds its natural home in the sacred waters of the Nile and is also represented as the central Goddess-form of the Denderah zodiac, from Het-heru's Temple of the same name; "The hieroglyph for this Hippopotamus was used for the heavens in general" and was also taken as a symbol of the stars of the constellation Draco, the Dragon [19], the constellation which with the Greater and Lesser Bears is the closest to the pole - star, the centre of heaven and the especial protector/guide of the Northern Hemisphere. A Goddess in Her own right, as Taur-t Ast, the Hippopotamus is the patroness of birth and mothers and may be fittingly invoked for protection in this regard. In relation to Denderah, called in Egyptian Ast au ab and *Ast aab-s Het-Her*: or the "Seat of the Heart" / "Seat of the Heart of Het-heru" [20] and reveals through this name the central importance of this symbol to life: the heart being the physical organ which all other organs and bodily functions depend upon and which spiritually contains the life and soul of the individual. Similarly, the Hippopotamus and Her stellar home of Draco, represents the centre of the celestial realm, around which all other stars revolve. Work with this aspect also for stellar illumination.

Lioness: as the representation of the fierce solar force, the Goddess Sekhmet is the patroness of martial activity, war, defence and warriors. Bloodthirsty and needing to drink, the Goddess was 'tricked' by the Sun-God Ra, Her father - whose Eye She also represented; into believing that jugs of pomegranate beer were blood and so drinking of them heavily and becoming drunk and sleeping, it is said that total destruction of mankind was prevented. Another less known work of Sekhmet is alluded to in the Black-Lioness statue forms in which She is known and this, like Bast, has reference to a Tuat aspect, where Sekhmet guards the papyrus scrolls which contain the life-deeds of each one. In this regard, She should be given utmost respect, for She is quite capable of devouring the unworthy.

On another note, the use of ritual drunkenness is a feature of Her worship and like Her beneficent counterpart, Het-heru; devotees and Priestesses of these solar aspects may find inspiration from the Goddess through an annual (not daily!) rite where a red beer is drunk freely. Patroness of 'red' work, the pomegranate beer and the fluids to which it alludes are indeed the source of both life, revitalisation and inspiration.

Scorpion: the only one of the four Goddess-Guardians of the canopic jars whose ideogram is in animal form, is Selket, also called Serquet; in this regard She may be invoked for protection. A complex lore revolving around the death-dealing venom wielded by this Goddess and through the power to heal through use of this venom is perhaps approachable, in one way, through a comparison with 'modern' homeopathy, where the cure is found within the cause and small amounts of bodily fluids are used to promote healing. That Ast has the power to heal the sting of the scorpion is revealed through th episode of Heru being bitten and subsequently healed by the Goddess and also in that Ast is depicted as having Seven Scorpions amongst Her entourage. The use of venom plays a prominent part in Ast's lore and finds further reference in regard to the use of a Serpent, fashioned from the dribble of the Sun-God Ra, to bite the God and require Ast to heal him. The use of venom is art magick of a particularly sacred nature, as it contains the powers of life and death. Work with this is auspiced under the Red Queen aspect and associated symbology of the Goddess Tabityt, sister-wife of Heru. (see "A Further Note...")

Swallow: a further solar transformation of Ast within the Tuat, the Swallow is distinguished with being the bird component, along with the mouth, of the hieroglyph for the word Great and the associated means of attaining greatness to rise. Through observation of Swallows in nature, it becomes apparent that they fly in a rapid upward motion and this is quite possibly the origin, within the Egyptian mind, of their suitability to denote this word. They fly very fast, rise quickly, dart and fly and rise again and again in a seemingly tireless pattern, which taking place amongst many other Swallows, also has a refreshingly light and playful appearance.

One of the lessons of this aspect is the need to be simultaneously focused straight ahead on a goal and yet not to take yourself too seriously, but to maintain a joyful engage-ment with life. The ability able to rise to meet any challenges, whilst still maintaining the ability to rise further is also suggested by the Swallow's flight. Ast when in this transformation, is often in the companionship of her sister Neb-t-het; with both Goddesses stationed at opposite ends of the Pharoah's sarcophagi enabling His spirit-soul to rise to renewed life. Work with this aspect is similar in end result to

Het-heru (i.e. patroness of mothers and birth)with focus on the ancestral regions.

On the Goddess' Transformations into the Animals of the Royal Insignia

The apparent paradox that the sovereign emblems of Upper and Lower Egypt, that is, the sacred Vulture and the Cobra are both necropolis dwellers and guardians, is resolved by an examination of the Egyptian view of life and death. That at death one returned to the ancestral abode to dwell with the gods and that this place was a blissful and peaceful one, where the daily needs of food and drink were met abundantly, is testified to both within the funerary hymns, coffin and tomb paintings and the prescribed offerings made to the dead. Both rich and poor alike returned to the Fields of Aaru if they passed the examination in the Judgement Hall and if their hearts were found to be pure.

Each successive Pharoah emerged from this blessed realm as the Osiris reborn. This continuum of existences and intimate interrelationship between the newly dead and the soon to be reborn provides the key to the understanding of why the Goddess in the manifestations of Her necropolis form, would be the choice for sovereign emblem: for she is both the nursing mother of the dead and the womb from which they re-emerged into a new life.

As with the other anthropomorphic forms of the Goddess, the attribution of sovereign power to the Vulture and the Cobra, was not coincidental, but followed centuries of profound observation and worship as the pre-eminent Goddesses of the pre-dynastic tribal groupings of the North (Cobra as Neith of Sais) and the South (Vulture as Nekhbet of Nekhen). In the shift from the local and independent cults to the centrally organised dynastic families, it was natural that these two ancient forms should be retained to represent the power of the newly emergent Kings of each of the Two Lands. However, over time, their importance was visually diminished, from the all-powerful Goddesses who ruled in their own right, to the small icon-like forms which adorned the crown of the Pharoah. In this way, these ancient and venerable powers became aligned to each Land as the Two Ladies,or the Two Mistresses; their hieroglyphic signs being shown above the ideogram 'neb-t' - the basket of bread /lady sign indicating the role as fecundating giver of life to land and the Pharoah's household.

The survival and dwelling of both Vulture and Cobra amongst the desolate and arid tomb areas of Egypt inspired both fear and respect in the ancients and was utilised to represent the awesome power of life sustained by death, or the double powers of life and death that each Pharoah wielded. Interestingly, both of the Two Ladies anciently were worshiped parthenogenic forms; that is, as being able to give birth (or, create) unaided. The mighty Cobra Goddess Neith, She who was and is the primordial Creatrix is anciently renowned in this capacity as self-creative and self-evident. The Vulture, Nekhbet, on the other hand was renowned for Her parthenogenic ability via Her spiral flight, said to create new life. It is apparent why the ability to be self-creative and master of the living and the dead would be powers each Pharoah would aspire to possess. As with other matters pertaining to the ancient Egyptian Kingship, the role of the feminine principle in empowering the male can be neither overlooked or denied.

Other subtler symbolism behind these divine manifestations of the Goddess include the dynamic interplay between the role of the mother (Vulture) and the daughter (Cobra) and the powers of regeneration attributed to the female principle in each of these manifestations. If you look closely at painted papyrus which contain female figures, you often will become aware that one wears a Vulture-headdress and another wears a Cobra-headdress, emblematic of the roles and powers outlined. As self-renewing and self-creative, both Cobra and Vulture were dually able to imbue the Pharoah with their fecund strength. It is in this renewal of life that an understanding of the underlying impetus within the Egyptian rites and the anthropomorphic representations of both goddesses and gods becomes clearer to modern minds and this quest for renewal is no less important today.

Hymn to Nekhbet

With vastness of gaze does the vulture fly and see Her prey
       from on high
No carrion will escape Her view
Upon the carcass She takes Her fill and
Having feasted well upon the dead
Will carry them back to life again. (2 a)

Hymn to Uadjet

Thy might is full spread on the ground
Unlike Her sister, She moves by sound
With hood raised does the piercing fang of Cobra send to the grave
With silence adore her potent form
Lest any vibration arouse, awake, alarm !
Full spread and raised, kiss Her majestic head
For She guards the living and suckles the dead. (21b)

So much of the majesty of the Egyptian religion and in understanding Isis is inextricably entwined with the features of the land,climate and animals which flourished in this environment, that it is no wonder that approaching the Goddess in any of Her more potent transformations may present difficulties to the modern, city-bred mind. What is required is the ability to think like the Egyptians and to try and grasp what each bird or animal meant to them within their land. Whilst this approach may also seem remote or fanciful (for how can an urban Twentieth Century mind think back to the mind-set of a people of 5,000 years ago?), it is still necessary to attempt to grasp this understanding, or it is impossible to find a modern relevance for these things. For example, to really work with the Goddess in Her animal Transformations, you need to be able to 'get into the mind-set' of the animal. Whilst this type of approach may be familiar to practitioners of Earth-based, totemic, or shamanic pathways; it is a point which has remained unemphasised, or unapparent to many seekers of the Egyptian wisdom, who may favour the human forms of the divine - as they appear more accessible. In this context, please keep in mind that it is within the animal-forms that the most ancient powers of the Goddess reside.

Without this important shift, in both consciousness and understanding, attempting to assume one of these forms for ritual work, often called backing into, or assuming the goddess/godform, will be a hollow experience. It is suggested as a useful approach, to obtain a good animal encyclopedia and research the habitats, diets, life-cycles and lifestyles of the various animals which are revered within the Egyptian system. Pay close attention to these details, for it was upon observation of these details that the ancient priesthood ascertained the most suitable earthly vehicle of the celestial powers. This point cannot be emphasised highly enough. All efforts you make to understand the particularities of each of the animals, will in turn give insights into the abilities and powers of an aspect of Ast and likewise with other Egyptian goddesses and gods who are also figured in animal-forms.

A Further Note On Sovereignty With Respect to the Two Ladies

Apart from the previous points, it must be emphasised that the ancient Egyptian language was full of subtle puns; the

Vulture Goddess, Sovereign Mother of Upper Egypt (the South), in Her name Nekhbet alluded to the important religious and secular role she played. Associated with the "nekh" part of Her name are ideas of "strength", "child", "to be young", and "death" [26]. It was clear to the ancients that the Vulture as a symbol was not morbid, decaying, or of mortality alone; but a symbol offering the hope of Life renewed. This is in fact, also explicit when Isis' name is spelt out fully, including the vowel 'A' which is represented by a bird hieroglyph, thought to be the Kite - a small Hawk in which form Ast became pregnant with Heru in the depths of the Tuat; in addition to the 'ST', or 'Throne' part of Her name. Due to the uncertainty of scholars regarding exactly what bird is portrayed, an interesting and symbolically appropriate possibility is that this bird is not a Kite, but a Vulture. If this is the case, then it is apparent that Ast is the 'Throne of the Vulture'; another way of interpreting this is that Her name means that She is the: Throne of Re-birth; Throne of Re-incarnation; the Seat of the Ancestral Return.

It is not only within the ancient Egyptian religion that the Vulture holds such a pre-eminent position, but also within the West Afrikan Tradition of the Yoruba peoples and the Ifa/Orisa Mysteries. Within this ancient and living Tradition, the Orisa Oshun manifests powerfully in one incarnation as a Vulture.; in this form She has responsibility for cleaning up and elevating the Spirit of the dead to the ancestors, ensuring that the energy may be received and in the appropriate time, be returned to Earth as an ancestor reborn.

This is also a role which Nekhbet - who literally scavenges the flesh off exposed carcasses and by consuming the meat incorporates it into her own Being; thus elevating it from the fleshy and physical to the Divine ancestral realms. This is one of the reasons that Nekhbet is sometimes portrayed as a Midwife; for from her, Re-birth is attained..

The emphasis on emblems of swift and sure death, such as the Cobra and the swift removal of the fleshy body after death, in the Vulture; are both suggestive of the way in which we each may attain a state of divine life.As the Cobra injects a poison, which is part of its own Being, into the flesh of one so bitten. Conversely, the Vulture consumes the flesh so destroyed, taking it into its own Being. A subtle talismanic reading of this, reveals that, the Divine Essence, that is, the Venom, is incorporated into the human vehicle, which is overwhelmed by this Divine force and so dies. Once the physical body is extinct, it is immediately consumed by the Vulture Queen, who carries the union of Divine Essence and ingested materium to the ancestors from where a rebirth upon Earth AS DIVINE becomes possible.

That this parallels the medieval alchemical processes, whereby the base material, the 'body', flesh, or earth, is altered, refined, purified and resurrected as an incorrupt GOLD, may be meaningful pointed out and meditated upon. That gold was also the physical material which the Egyptians chose to manifest the Sovereign emblems is again highly significant. The gold Cobra and the gold Vulture both symbolise and embody potently the processes of alchemy; not only the black, but also the red and the white. The resultant 'Philosopher's Stone' - able to transmute all things to gold, creates important parallels upon which a deeper understanding of the power of the Two Ladies may be uncovered. The gold Vulture pectoral, so omnipresent upon and wholly covering the upper chest (and Heart area) of the unearthed royal personages, is thus both a sign of protection, elevation of the deceased to the ancestral realm and also a glyph of re-birth.

Of importance then in this process and central to ancient Egyptian belief and view of these emblems - is the promise that each person upon death will become the 'Osiris..' reborn upon the wings of the Vulture Mother.

In wearing the Cobra/Vulture during life, each Pharoah proclaimed not only their divinity, but that they were a 'reborn one' - crowned with the signs of power, of transformation, of the divine in human form; all these may be meditated upon to aid in understanding the transformative powers contained within the emblems; a consciousness that Vulture and Cobra embody the primary powers that may be harnessed in both life and death is another way of assimilation.

Carefully and respectfully approached, Nekhbet may also be honoured as a primary Tutelary Goddess of re-birth; One who has the Power to Transform each one of us from 'lead' to 'gold' and She also possesses the Strength to carry us home in this quest, from the old, into a new and renewed life.

That Pharoah, Queens, Gods and Goddesses alone wore these emblems of absolute authority and power upon their Crown, also points to Greater Mysteries, befitting the roles each one played as the Highest Priest/Priestess incarnating their Divine ancestors. To other High Initiates; a Crown displaying one or both emblems would be understood through the personal experience of these powers which the senior Priests/Priestesses would have encountered in their Training.

To an Initiate of a lower rank and also to the population in general, the Two Ladies, when displayed upon Pharoah's Crown, would ever remain symbols of awesome power, perhaps sometimes taken quite literally, defying the comprehension of the average Egyptian; this was authority not to be questioned.

However, as with all symbols and mysteries, their subtlety and complexity only comes to Light through use and this is suggestive of the playing out of Initiatic ritual Dramas, deep within the Temple, perhaps at a Necropolis site to evoke the mysteries of the Night. In such an Initiatory Cycle, a

Candidate of the lesser Mysteries could be led to a direct experience of the higher powers and a transformation of psyche effected.

Calling to mind the Egyptian use of punning within language and the Outer and Inner meanings alluded to by such puns; the 'venom' the Cobra emits could be interpreted as a preparation, perhaps of animal, plant or herb extracts, which the Candidate would ingest - inducing an experience of personal 'death; i.e. loss of ego. This may have included being taken on a 'flight' of some kind, where the Candidate saw themselves ascending via a Vulture and then being Reborn. Such a ritual cycle, involving use of a consciousness-altering substance, or 'venom'; a vision of 'death'; a 'flight' and subsequent re-birth, accord with the Traditional patterns of many Shamanic Initiations; where it is essential for Mastery of Greater Forces, to cease revering those powers as external deity, but have full experience of containing those powers within.

The shifts of consciousness suggested by the roles of Cobra - an earthly vehicle containing and transmitting a potentially lethal substance; the human, or Candidate in the Mysteries who receives the Cobra's venom and the Sky and Earth vehicle of Vulture, who has the double role of both consuming the venomous flesh and transmuting the poison to enable rebirth upon the Earth.

In this connection, both Serpent and Bird hold great significances, again in many other ancient cultures - as symbols of eternal rebirth and the power to transform and shift states of consciousness.

In this Cycle, the interplay of the primal coupling of Earth (Geb) and Sky (Nut) - producing the Five Divine Children is represented through the Being of Earth (Serpent) and the Being of Air (Vulture). Working together as twin mechanisms, they produce a third thing - a transformed, transmuted

Divine Consciousness. There are other important significances to this pairing, further of which are discussed in the
Chapter "Lighting The Lamps".

That such an Initiatory Cycle was enacted as the Gateway
between the Outer (Lesser) and Inner (Greater) Mysteries is
substantiated, not only by a careful study of the patterns
within the Outer Mysteries, but also through a study of the
funerary texts such as sequence both in life and in death. It
was perhaps, the conscious accessing of those realms during
life - gaining the familiarity with the paths which would
ensure the success of the journey - after death.

The use of the word 'venom' as a pun concealing secondary
allusions to magickal substances with both life-transformative
potency and visionary potential needs to be considered open-
mindedly.

With their wide and skillful knowledge of medicinal plants
and herbs - to the point of being able to preserve the human
body after death, it is not inconceivable that a substance was
known and in use which enabled the type of journeying just
discussed. That the *"Book Of Going Forth By Day"* and other
funerary texts contains such a detailed and careful mapping
of realms of existence, in all respects parallel realms to ours;
as well as revealing the means of approach and type of terrain
encountered both before and after death, adds weight to this
suggestion. It would have taken many generations of a Highly
Initiated Priesthood, many ritual journeys to map out these
terrains - which on one level can be understood as descriptive
of the changes (both chemical, electrical, physical and
spiritual) which take place within and to consciousness at the
time of death and also at the time of falling asleep: at these
times, consciousness separates from the body and may
journey, unencumbered, to loftier realms. Death, may be
considered from both a literal physical and a symbolic and
spiritual context.

However, an additional point when considering the pivotal role that 'venom' plays in this process, is that it is a living substance from within a Divine source. This again parallels the 'alchemical Stone', so often called a 'Living Stone'. Implied within this, is that only life, may transmit life and the knowledge and the processes of life.

That such a 'venom' can be constructed, utilising magickal knowledge, is specified within Ast's Traditional Lore; where She makes a Giant Serpent, utilising Her magickal skills and spells, in combination with a small portion of a 'living substance' - the God Ra's own 'saliva'. With this Serpent (and fashioned out of His own substance) Ra is bitten and poisoned; it is only through use the power of His Own name - sending its power into Ast's body - that he gains access to Ast's 'antivenom' healing powers.

Here, it is essential to remember that 'venom' is also obtained from an additional source within the Egyptian Rites - the Goddess Selket, the Scorpion. That Ast possesses the power of this 'venom' also' is again explicitly stated; for at one point Heru is bitten by a Scorpion, falling sick and Ast heals him of this sting.

Two distinct magickal powers are here detailed, as is the means of their operation:

> 1. The ability to create, or construct, an edible Talisman, utilising ur heka and a fragment of biological material - with 'death-inducing' properties.

> 2. The ability to overpower the 'death-dealing' aspect and effect healing and the maintenance of a renewed life.

Within Ast's Lore, as befits a Mistress Of Magick, are possessed the powers to both create 'venom' & 'antivenom'; these again echo the powers of Life and Death contained within the Sovereign emblems. A suggestion within this, is that, the practitioner must be highly skilled in the knowledge and preparation of consciousness-altering elixirs and rites and be able to effect a Renewal of Life within their work and through participation in such Rites. This also includes the ability to both Descend (Serpent) and Ascend (Vulture), journeying to the powerful ancestral realms. These are points that should be kept in mind when reaching the later Chapters dealing with this.

However, as the ancient Egyptian priesthood so meticulously mapped their journeyings; it is for us to find the ways to follow amongst the carefully detailed routes. These exist in their own right, as constructed anciently as archetypal abodes and also exist within each Aspirant in an individual and subjective manner, 'coloured' or 'personalised' by our own life's path. We may, briefly and without deliberation, access this subjective realm within our own deep mind, when we dream and 'astral travel'. That the Two Ladies were both revered and feared by the people in general, also points to a Guardian of these Inner Places of Power and the need to be willing to journey very deep indeed in order to begin to unravel the meticulous patterns inherent within the Egyptian Mysteries.

Whilst the use of 'venom' may appear strange or repugnant to a Western mind; it has been literally and effectively employed by Traditional Cultures and Shaman-in-training since ancient times. An example of this is found within the Native American Tradition and in particular, Initiates whose Totem is Snake medicine - supposedly rare - as the Initiation involves repeated bites of venomous snakes, which the Shaman must internally transmute and survive(see Jamie Sams' "Medicine Cards"). It goes without saying, that such medicine people are very powerful indeed.

Whilst not explicitly stated within 'popular' Egyptian texts; the use of Cobra Venom, in a diluted form as a ritual potion to induce a death-trance and then hallucinatory flight and re-birth experience has an Inner Tradition and certainly holds potent magickal symbolism and power, which should be understandable in Light of the foregoing discussion.

It is perhaps to this use that Cleopatra alerts us, if we listen and look carefully at the retelling of the story of Her death. As Queen and thus as the Highest Priestess of Isis (Ast), Cleopatra would have been privy to both the direct experience and understanding of the Greater Mysteries of which She would have enacted the role of the Goddess Isis Herself. Ast as Mistress Of Magick and possessing both the power of the Serpent (Venom) and the Scorpion (Venom), has been outlined. Perhaps it was to this form, which Cleopatra either assumed or invoked as She placed the Royal Serpent to Her heart - forcing it to bite Her, injecting its venom - ensuring both a swift and suitably royal and magickally evocative death; but also ensuring an equally swift integration into the body of the Great Mother, Nekhbet (Ast in another form) and rebirth. In this way Cleopatra returned Herself to her divine state and source, with the aid of the Earthly incarnation of that force, the Serpent - ensuring Her rebirth as Divine Child.

That Cleopatra's means of death have been retold by both ancient writers and also by Shakespeare in short narrative - and most importantly *without comment* i.e. that this was an incomprehensible act for a Queen, is very revealing.

The means by which Cleopatra chose to end her life befitted a Queen; for it contains both Initiated symbolism, outward Sovereign Authority and guaranteed an afterlife/rebirth.

It is my suggestion, that her death reveals both an Initiated Knowledge and a familarity with the patterns of 'death' and 'trance-death' associated with the ingestion of the Venom.

This literal use of 'venom' as a substance within certain Rites, the Knowledge of the uses of which formed a part of the Greater Mysteries (as would the identity of the 'antivenom').In modern times the (re) discovery that 'like' cures 'like', may also have been well-known anciently. All venoms are proteins, which act upon specific sites, either muscle, nerve, or neuro-transmitters: depending on the dose a physical paralysis accompanied by out-of -body hallucinations for a length of time, could quite feasibly have been utilised as an Initiatory sacrament, with profound effects. This does not discount that this type of effect could and may also be induced with the use of 'other venoms'.

That a *Divine Name* contains the power which the Goddess acquires in exchange for unleashing Her healing 'antivenom', is also noteworthy. The parallels between, the Old god Ra being poisoned by the Serpent and the Young God Heru being poisoned by a Scorpion, are also keys: Serpent = 'Ancient', Scorpion = 'Youthful', perhaps also alluding to the strengths or 'potency' of the 'venom'. This is suggestive of the interplay between Father-Son / Mother - Daughter; the forms of rejuvenation between the older and younger Gods.

Within the Greater Mysteries, perhaps the entire symbol of Cobra/Vulture points to the revitalisation of magickal power and renewal of life-force as being sourced within the consumption of a living, liquid talisman.

When represented visually, again the pattern is clear; the central and united powers enable the process and exactly mirror the patterns apparent within both the Daily and the Annual Rites: as within these, the entire land is traversed and glyphed in another form as are the Three Realms of earth, Sky and Tuat and the Three Seasons:

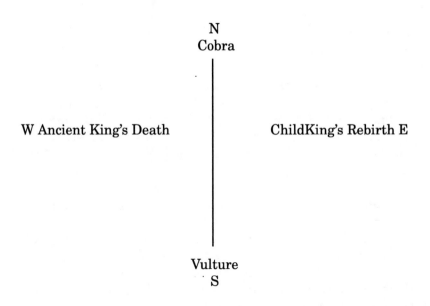

This may all be usefully summarised as: Cobra bite injects venom - leading to a return to Godhead - via the Gate of the Underworld.

That these correspondences provide ceremonial formulae which may be usefully applied to such things as the setting up and alignment of a Temple space and also contain keys to enable each one to be led to a direct experience of these ancient mysteries, is perhaps the clearest means of approaching this vast and rich metaphor.

Whilst it has been emphasised in all the foregoing, that the ancient connection of Ast was pre-eminently with the Throne of the Pharoah; it must now also be emphasised that the relationship each Pharoah had with His 'Throne' was tenuous. It was his only marriage to his Elder Sister and subsequent adoption - both his by the Goddess and the Goddess by him - for in wearing the Sovereign emblems each Pharoah was enabled to assume power and ascend the Throne - a Seat of divine power never empty for the Vulture Goddess ever abides there.

The significance of the placement of these emblems upon his brow, points also to an alignment of power within the Two Lands through him. Referring to the previous diagram, if a human body, say the body of Pharoah, was transposed upon the Lands, then the position of both Vulture and Cobra become both significant and suggestive. The axis between Upper and Lower Egypt within the literal landscape, is composed of the flowing Nile and the fertile lands which fall immediately upon either side of it. This river, a Divine Being, unites and energises the Two Lands in both an inner and outer way. In some ways, its role can be likened to the roles that both blood and the central nervous system play within the body; most tangible in the spinal column, with its pivotal position and ascending and descending transmissions.

If we locate the South (Vulture) as the feet; this as a base of the body's central energy system can also be aligned to the base of the spine. Then North (Cobra) is located at the head - the place where the Sovereign emblems were worn. But if these things are interpreted as the symbols which they are and always have been, then it is striking how the alignment of the Two Lands accords with explanations given for the highest illumination - sourced within the internal experience of the Kundalini Serpent ascending, via the Chakras located in the spinal area, to the Ajna Chakra - the Inner Eye of Vision and then on to the Crown Chakra - giving illumination. The wearing of the Sovereign emblems together, is because the Two Lands fall beside each other and forms an abbreviated glyph of Unity and the enormous power of both the land itself and of Pharoah's body as a microcosm of that power. That the Two Ladies co-jointly ruled over both lands after the Unification leads also to the natural dispositioning of both Cobra and Vulture in the reverse and alternate positions of Cobra at feet (base of spine) and Vulture at head.

This again can be interpreted in terms of Kundalini movement and perhaps is the position and glyph for the beginning
of the movement of power, or of the conscious use and
manifestation of such power. The assignment of Vulture as
Mother and Cobra as Daughter when viewed in terms of these
positions contains additional insights; Vulture at the brow is
an undeniable Outer symbol of maturity and Wisdom, much
as Cobra at the base of the spine presents a sign of immense
and available energy. Other interpretations could be made by
practitioners of Yoga, familiar with Kundalini symbolism;
with the Goddess, when Crowned with the Cobra alone, seen
to be Kundalini Herself.

The potent and complex lore of the Goddess Ast's Transformations fittingly ends upon that note and upon reflection, is
seen as not just an 'important point' within the Egyptian
Tradition, but as perhaps, the most important and profound
reservoir of its timeless wisdom.

3. Temple Service

Within the ancient Egyptian Temples a strictly regulated
hierarchy of priests and priestesses fulfiled their duties and
were classed according to both the duration of office and the
functions they performed. The notion of the priestly life was
and is pre-eminently that of service, as the hieroglyphs used
generically to denote both a priest *hem neter* and a priestess
hem-t neter [16] may both be translated to mean "servant of the
divine"; *neter* being the word used to denote the divine and
creative realm, the gods and goddesses, that which is a sacred
mystery. An additional and interesting feature of the word
hem-t neter, is that it was also utilised to denote the rank of
one who was a wife of the god [17] alluding to other aspects
which a senior, or High Priestess' role may entail. This class
of Priestess functioned at the closest and highest levels to the
incarnate god, the Pharoah and to his representative and was
often filled by his own sister-wife and close female relations.

often filled by his own sister-wife and close female relations. Only Goddesses such as Ast, who were married within the divine hierarchy and legends, were also permitted to have the hem-t neter class of priestess in their Temple service and several Priestesses of this Red aspect also served within the Temples of Het-heru (Hathor), Selket, Tabityt, Asar and Heru. Apart from this more generalised priestly title, other titles in common usage included hem neter tepi - a high priest; hem or hem-t ankhiu - "servant of the living" [18] and titles which were directly connected to a specific role in ritual; such as the priests involved in the various stages of the funerary rites and offerings.

The view that the priestly role was a permanent one, or perhaps a 'career path', is in many cases misleading; whilst their were both male and female Temple servitors who were such for life, there were a far greater number who were part of the regularly rotated groups who performed their duties on a seasonal roster basis. These priests and priestesses were of a lower class and had to attend the Temple for only certain periods of each year; such as one month out of every four, of sometimes for three months consecutively - the remainder of the year they were free to resume their individual home-lives, including marriage, children and agricultural activities. Whilst this custom may at first seem unusual, given the intense activities and demands of the Temple Service, it was a very practical means of ensuring that both the sacred and secular domains were well cared for.

During the period of Temple Service a rigorous discipline was maintained. The Temple awoke around 4am (pre-dawn) each day and the various groups began their work. This included the making of all the Temple's requirements: including the baking of the loaves of bread and preparing the vast offering trays that were taken in at dawn. The amount of work was enormous and skilled craftspeople in attendance at the Temple also included builders, artists, jewellers and potters.

Prior to the first service of the day, the Dawn Service; all priestesses and priests would prepare for the morning by thorough purification rites which included bathing in the lake adjacent to the Temple, washing the mouth with natron, removing all bodily hair and robing in a pure white linen garment. The removal of all bodily hair was strictly enforced and fines were laid on any of the priestly class not properly shaved. In the hot Egyptian climate, these daily bathing and shaving rituals were a practical means to promote bodily purity and good health and prevented any vermin on the body. It was also a means of showing submission to the divine realm which one served.Ceremonial wigs and headdresses were then worn by women, whilst men remained clean shaven. These customs may be easily adapted for solo or group use with a bath filled with fresh water, salt and appropriate herbs for the work about to be undertaken being steeped in the bath. Whilst there may be no fines today for not being fully body-shaved, it should be kept in mind what the Egyptian deities prefer and if one is sincere in working within their Temple, then perhaps some deep thought on this issue should be made individually and a means of accommodating this portion of the principle of bodily purity can then be made. It is apparent in any case, that a minimum of the body being freshly bathed (e.g. showered) and cleanly robed is a pre-requisite for entering the shrine.

It is interesting too, the emphasis on the mouth being washed with natron, prior to commencing the Dawn service. This ritual action features in the Dawn Service itself, when the mouth of the statue of the goddess or god is similarly bathed. This cleansing preceded the pronouncement of *ur heka* - those words of magick and hymns of praise which are efficacious in Opening the Shrine and symbolised the requirement that the utterance of the priestesses and priests always be pure, that is true, or Maat - without such Truth no word or work would find success or blessing within the Temple and by extension, within life. The importance of adhering to this principle has in no way diminished today for those who aspire to work within Ast's Temple, or within the Temples of other Egyptian powers; in fact, given the state of affairs in the external world, this is an aspect of the ancient service that may need to be focused on with a greater intent, for the disregard for truth and the concealment of truth has become almost a characteristic of this time we live in.

Following the bathing and robing, all classes of priests would assemble in the courtyard and begin carrying the trays of hetepu neter into the sanctuary, led by the highest priest or priestess. Once inside, it was only the highest official who began the long walk in the semi-darkness down the narrow corridor which led to the door of the Inner Shrine, where the statue of the Goddess dwelt. There,in private, the Dawn Rites would commence: the Shrine would be Opened and the statue of the Goddess placed upon the altar; the purification of the Goddess' mouth with natron; anointing of the Goddess; robing in the sacred fabrics and the making of hetepu neter accompanied by the singing of various litanies of power. The Goddess being thus awakened and having satisfied Herself of the offerings, the officiant was then able to take a portion of the foods for their own consumption. This ancient precedent may be followed with success today and so it may be said that the priestly class are 'fed upon the table of the divine'. Abuse of this practise occurred anciently and must also be avoided today - the divine must be truly satisfied before any of the food is removed for consumption, to enable communion with its essence.

Once the Dawn rite was completed, the priestly classes were free to pursue individual activities until the Noon Rite - as the Temple day was divided into ritual activities regulated by the solar phases: Rising in the East, the Dawn Rite; Crossing the Heavens to its highest point, the Midday Rite; Setting in the West, the Sunset Rite; then the various rites of the Hours of the Night the am Tuat, which found their pinnacle at Midnight. It is unlikely that any one priest or priestess officiated at all these rites around the clock; although at certain important times of the year such as will be detailed later, all observances would have been kept for the period of the ritual cycle. The difference in the ritual energy at each of these times is noticeable, as is their suitability for different types of sacred activity.

The Dawn Rite represents the time when the Solar disc, having successfully traversed the regions of the Tuat, the ancestral realms, during the hours of the night - emerges triumphant via the Eastern portal to begin its ascent across the sky. This corresponds to spiritual awakening, birth of aspiration and the gods and the time of the Spring Equinox.

Having continued to rise in the morning sky to a point of balanced height, the Midday Rite represents the time of maximum achievement and force - which may be used to promote life and growth (Het-heru) or for more destructive results (Sekhmet). At this point, both the solar ability to create and to destroy are seen as complementary powers and hence the symbolism of the fecundating solar principle within one Goddess and the burning and destroying solar principle is within Her other aspect. This corresponds to the experience of conscious existence, outer strength and Summer Solstice.

Having traversed the sky and descended, the Sunset Rite represents the time when the Solar Disc goes, via the Western portal, into Amen-t; there to begin its journey through the regions of the Tuat during the hours of the night. This corresponds to the experience of unconscious existence, inner strength and Autumn Equinox.

Once inside the Tuat, the Solar disc is within the womb of night, within the night-sky body of the great ancestress goddess Nut, firstborn of the primordial Chaos and darkness.

In this place of timelessness and yet all-time is the realm of the ancestors. The journey through the hours of the am Tuat corresponds to outer space (as in the stellar realms) and to inner space (the parts of our brain and nervous system which are capable of receiving information from this realm), also dream-visions and the time of Winter Solstice.

Both the life of the Goddess, via Her statue and the life of the Temple servitors - the priestesses and priests partake in these cycles: as the statue of the god was awakened and raised in the morning, able to accomplish its work throughout the day and then returned to its state of rest in the evening, so too do is the experience of those who serve the divine realm.

These ancient patterns of Temple Service may be adapted for contemporary usage and offer a means to connect the consciousness of the practitioner with the consciousness of other realms.

Daily Rites should be maintained by Initiates of the Priesthood; whilst weekly and monthly rites, on days suited to the aspects being worked with, may be utilised effectively to enhance the understanding and progress of all aspirants. The importance in establishing and maintaining a regular work within the Temple, enables a gradual building up of the levels of potency. A suggested allocation of Isis' aspects to days of the week has already been made in the previous chapter. The construction of the Temple and a suggested way to establish a modern shrine and ritual space now follows.

The first step is to select a location, within your own house - an accessible and practical suggestion, acknowledging that few today would have the finances available to purchase/rent a separate facility for their spiritual activity. A most important feature of the location, whether it be large or small, is that it is loved - to understand why this is important, return to the list of the Hieroglyphic names of the Goddess and you will discover that Ast's primary Temples have always been denoted as either *Ast au ab* or *Ast uab*: Her "Seat of the Heart" or Her "Holy Place".

The *ab* or heart as a key of power and the location of life, will be returned to. First, it is essential to the creation of a sacred place of power that it be aligned to eternal principles. Through creating a space in accordance with the ancient Egyptian classification of the different parts of a person, a natural resonance of self with beloved, as embodied within the Temple, may be achieved. As the Temple, or Shrine, becomes a literal and physical manifestation of spiritual power, so it is akin to the human body khat, an outer form which is liable to decay; this outer body has a spiritual form a sahu which is eternal and inviolate and accords with the belief that the astral reality of a Temple is that which ever remains.

Accompanying both the khat and the sahu is the part of a person which moves through both the physical and the spiritual realms as a person's spiritual genius and double, this is the ka and a different sign was used to denote a male or a female ka. Animating the life of the individual are the ab, or heart and the ba, the eternal heart-soul, which has the power to reanimate the life of the *ab*. The ability 'to go forth', to move unhindered, is supplied by day (*khat* and *ab*) and by night (*sahu*, *ba* and *ka*). Beyond the physical aspects of a person and these spiritual correlatives exist the aspects of both light, the *khu* and of dark, the *khaibit*. Importantly, this recognition that the whole and fully animated person was comprised of not only flesh and spirit, but also a shining and a shadow presence. This offers a wholistic world-view and one which embraces the full dynamic, without relegating either light or dark to a superior or inferior role.

The value of examining what each person was understood to be composed of by the ancient Egyptians, lays in the pattern this offers for the construction of a Temple - which also is a living and animated 'body' housing the Divine - this view of the Temple is emphasised by its Egyptian title *het neter*: literally meaning 'house of the Gods'. As with many other words, *neter* denotes a range of important principles; primary of which is the divine, creative, sacred realm. To properly construct a modern and personal *het neter* for use in the service of the *neter Ast*, each 'layer' of its 'body' must be taken into account.

Returning to the selection of location, as stated above, this must be in a room that is 'loved'; the most easy way to think of this is that you would not choose a room which you disliked or had a strong negative feeling about as the location to construct your Shrine. The words 'shrine' and 'temple' have been used fairly interchangeably in this Chapter and will continue to be so used, keeping in mind that a 'Shrine' may be a smaller intimate sacred space for you to enter the presence of the Goddess alone; whilst a 'Temple' may hold several distinct 'Shrines' for specific aspects/forces and also may be large enough to accommodate other participants in ceremony. What you construct will undoubtedly be the result of a combination of available and suitable 'loved' space and your personal spiritual aspiration. Also, in choosing the location, keep in mind the many functions that the ancient Temples served and which a modern Temple may also serve on a personal scale; the existence of myriad Shrines and Temples of many sizes, some as small as a the size of finger and worn by a devotee, have perhaps remained unknown and overshadowed by the might and majesty of the famous Pyramids and related Temples.

If you are fortunate enough to have a room which may be set aside solely for spiritual activities, this would serve as a good place to locate the Temple; on the other hand, if you have limited space, a small section of a room may be devoted to the service of the *neter*.

Several things to consider when selecting a space:

1.Egyptian Temples are rectangular.

2.There is no need for external light (e.g. a window, unless you are orientating your Shrine to the movement of a particular celestial body which is visible through the window).

3.Orientation of the Temple follows the daily movement of the Sun and the alignment of the Two Lands.

4.Quadrants may be highlighted at the upper corners of the room - the symbolic space where Earth and Sky meet, this practise is observable in the ancient Temples as the ornate pillars adorned with Lotus (plant emblem of Upper Egypt) and the Papyrus (plant emblem of Lower Egypt). The elemental directions of these quadrants are aligned to the orientation of the physical land of Egypt _ for it is upon these that the true inner meanings of the neter come to life:

East = Fire (i.e Rising Sun); South =Earth (Upper Land): West = Air (i.e Desert); North = Water (i.e Lower Egypt heading out to the Mediterranean Sea). This is one of the reasons that the Altar may be usefully placed in the East.

Point #1. above is critical and needs further comment, particularly as the widespread use of the Circle as a ceremonial form and Circle-casting is a very well-known means of delineating sacred space.It must be emphasised that this is inappropriate to Egyptian Rites and was not in use within the ancient Egyptian Temples as sacred space once established within a permanent locale of a properly founded Shrine, is maintained at a very high tension through regular usage. The Circle, a very portable Temple and in every way commensurate with the internal energy and aura of the practitioner who 'casts' it; is a geometric sign of great power utilized in other ways within the Egyptian Rites. Within these Rites, the body of the practitioner and the Temple are synonymous with each other, in accordance with the ancient principles just expressed regarding the body. It becomes very true, that a mark of the spiritual health and the energy of the Shrine, may be measured by the health and energy of the practitioner - once established, all work performed within the Shrine energises not only the neter, but also the life of the one performing the work. This interconnection is explicit within the interrelationships between the *khat, sahu, ka, ab, ba, khu* and *khabaits* - all aspects of a person, both physical and spiritual require continued tending and feeding to ensure the continued maintenance of life.

A development of consciousness of these subtle bodies which exist within each one of us is highly recommended and becomes essential to fuller comprehension of the ways in which the Temple is energised. As the khat forms the physical and outer shell manifesting the individual life; does the ab form the physical-spiritual centre the Heart is the pivotal point of the entire physical-spiritual existence and is of such immense importance that not only the life and well-being of the individual - both in this life and the next - as well as the spiritual intelligence of the individual is housed here. It is in all respects the Sun of Our Solar System. This ancient knowledge is of immense importance to us today; including the ability to treat physical ailments by ascertaining their underlying spiritual cause/s. When both establishing and maintaining a Shrine this principle must be kept firmly in mind and also helps to explain the central role which the Heart plays in the Judgement Hall before the Assessors of the Dead. In this last connection, the role of the Goddess Maat, incarnate within Her Feather, in relation to the Heart, is also worth contemplating prior to establishing a Shrine - for the works which you perform within it and upon its spiritual heart, the Altar, will indeed be ultimately assessed in the Light of the Truth which they demonstrate -or not.

Nothing sacred, which is real, is ever performed without the full knowledge and watchful gaze of those whom we seek to invoke.

Having cleaned and charged the space as preliminary steps; now place a large lighted candle at the centre of the room. As you light this candle, visualize that you are lighting a flame which has its origins in Egypt itself, that its light is drawn from the first ray of Dawn Sunlight, the first ray of Moonlight and the first ray of Starlight to ever hit the Two Lands. See this light as being intimately connected to yourself, to your own highest will and as radiating out from the light at the centre of your being within your heart. Offer a heartfelt prayer to the ancient powers of Egypt and ask that the Goddess bless your effort to construct a worthy Shrine to Her. It is unnecessary to perform any other work, at this stage, until you have acquired the necessary items to build the Altar. Ensure that the candle is in a safe receptacle and allow it to burn, unhindered. Replace this candle each day until you are ready to commence constructing the Altar.

The Lighting of this Light has both ancient precedence and potent symbolism and should be reflected upon.

When you are ready to establish the Altar, you will need either a large piece of stone or timber for an Altar-top and some form of small chest or cupboard to place it upon; this will serve the additional purpose of enabling storage of sacred materials when not in use. Candleholders, candles, the censor and incense, a picture or even better, a statue of the Goddess and other symbolic objects associated with Her that you may wish to consecrate to the Shrine now (or can be obtained later), a clean and new piece of white linen to wear and a large quantity of fresh food and drink for the Feast at the end. This Ceremony will take quite a while so ensure that you will not be disturbed. Choose candle colours, incense, food and drink from the colours etc as listed in the Hetepu neter section of this book. Assemble all things outside the room and have a ritual bath before commencing. As noted previously, bathing is an essential step before entering the Temple and one which was always done by the priesthood.

At this point it should be noted, that while you are constructing, gathering and assembling all these things, you are also in effect, gathering and assembling yourself for a sacred purpose. Once you have bathed, robe yourself in the clean white linen, open the door to the Shrine (if there is one) and enter. Once inside notice the immediate details of the atmosphere - how has it altered since the preliminary sweeping, cleaning and charging?

Stand at the centre, breathe deeply to regularize your breathe and then state out loud: your name (secular or if you use one, magickal); your intention and purpose - be descriptive and try to fully state your reasons for establishing a sacred space; humbly request the assistance and blessing of higher powers in your quest - but do not at this stage invoke anything/anybody; pause and if you feel you have approval to continue, light the central candle, hold it aloft and requesting the blessing of both Sky and Earth - place it upon the floor again.

It will be noticed that no words have been given to 'recite' whilst you perform this - as this is your personal Shrine, the sentiments should originate deep within you and reflect your understanding and commitment to what you are doing. If you cannot think of anything to say, perhaps consider if this is really the right time. The utterance of words of power and truth - from the heart - have a potent effect in opening up sources of guidance.

Now go outside and carry the material basis you have chosen to construct the Altar from, into the Shrine and set about turning it into a functional Altar. The same preliminary steps (cleansing and charging and statement of intention) also need to be performed over and to the Altar, once it is in place.The next important step, is the installation of the Goddess in Her Shrine; any picture or statue of the Goddess, should be carried into the Shrine in an upright and dignified manner. This accords with the ancient pattern of making a processional walk with the statue of a divinity from where it was fashioned into the inner recesses of the Temple. Once inside, the statue must be bathed and charged, as was the room, your body and the altar; however, as this is a statue of a Goddess, water may be substituted with rose water (obtainable at many stores). Carefully bathe the Goddess from head to toe and then robe Her in an appropriate fabric depending on the aspect the statue portrays however gold fabric is suitable in all cases. Now place Her upon Her Altar and add candles each side and other items as applicable to your personal aesthetic.

Stand back form the Altar and observe the outer form, that all is in harmony; make adjustments if necessary.

Return to the centre of the space and now is the time to perform the Shrine Opening (see "Ur heka " Chapter). At each point in the Opening, visualize the forces called upon as clearly and as intensely as is possible. If necessary, before undertaking this, if you are unsure, familiarize yourself with the details of these powers by researching in books on ancient Egypt that contain colour pictures and then practise visualizing them out of a ritual context until you feel competent. Obviously, this is an aspect of what you will and do in the Shrine which will become stronger and more meaningful, with the potential for real transformation of consciousness (i.e magick) with practise.

Declare the Shrine Open and if you have chosen one, give it (i.e your work) a name. Along with the Shrine's *khat* - its outer form and its sahu - its spiritual (astral form); along with its *ab* - the Altar and its *ba* - the spiritual (astral) correlative of the altar and all that is upon it and igniting the 'flame', the luminescent *khu* and its corresponding shadow, the *khabaits*; the other single most important aspect of an individual existence and by extension of metaphor, the existence and life of the Shrine, is its name.

The name of anything was accorded such importance by the ancients, that there was a very real reluctance to give out a real name. This is why each Pharoah was given a series of three major names when he ascended the Throne, one was for use as a personal and outer name, another, his Throne name and another a spiritual name. The belief that the name housed a potent part of the life of an individual that could be possessed if the real inner name was known, is forcefully demonstrated within Ast's Traditional lore in the tale of Her acquiring the name of the old Sun-God Ra and thereby attaining His powers.

In choosing a spiritual (magickal) name for either yourself of your Shrine, consider the implications of that name, both anciently (if applicable) - for this carries any collected power/ and or 'karma' associated with the name, presently and for the future - does the name carry /express your aspirations in establishing the Shrine?

A name, once given/chosen and used regularly becomes a personal identifier, a form of 'calling card' that is issued upon the air and from there, transmitted straight to the realm of the neter. It is also worth thinking about whether you would wish to have an 'outer' and an 'inner' name for either yourself or your Shrine. Once selected, state this name at and over the altar. Other means of charging a name to a particular act of will may also be utilised.

Having cleansed and charged the space and everything in it and awakened it with a Rite of Opening and Naming; it is time to ground all this activity into a consumable talisman - a feast. Offer all foods and drink in a festive display before the Goddess and offer a song of praise (see "Ur heka"). When you feel that this offering has been accepted, remove the best portion of everything presented onto a separate plate and give to the Goddess and do not touch this plate again (until it is removed from the Shrine).

At this point you may partake of the foods and drink and as you do so, concentrate on not only the outer form of what you consume, but the spiritual reality of this food and its ability to strengthen your links with the Shrine and with you higher purpose. As you so nourish the Shrine, so too will you be nourished. Once the feast is completed - and please note, that whilst certain of the Goddess' Festivals do contain ritual debauch (e.g. certain of both Het-heru and Sekhmet celebrations) - this is a solemn and important time and not an occasion for either overconsumption, or drunkenness - Close the rite with a simple statement of thanksgiving, allowing the candles to burn down of their own accord.

Often candles will be left burning in the Shrine for long periods unattended (such as during the Lychnapsia) and it is vital that this may be done safely and without risk of causing damage. Choosing generous-sized candle-holders/ a flame-proof (e.g. stone) Altar are two ways of creating a safe environment for the candles. Not extinguishing Lights during certain rituals serves several distinct purposes: 1. Enables the power generated within the Shrine to remain linked with the consciousness of the practitioner - this is of immense and potent use particularly for obtaining dream oracles. 2. Enables the Goddess to be illuminated for long period, with the resultant benefits. 3. Enables a rite to be maintained for a longer period of time - the duration of a ceremony commencing when a flame is lit and usually the end usually signalled by it being extinguished 4. a perpetual-burning flame represents and symbolizes the devotion and aspiration of the practitioner and this should be ever bright and finally 5. accords with a portion of the negative confession; which each one must be able to swear to pass through the Judgement Hall; namely, that one has not extinguished a flame when it should burn. This also implies the use of discrimination and spiritual intelligence on the behalf of the practitioner in deciding at which times of the year and for which purposes, candles should be left alight.

For those experienced in other forms of ritual work, it will be noticed that there are not any 'banishings' performed at the Close of this ceremony and the reason is simple and clear: you have just spent all this effort in cleansing and charging and installing and naming a space, establishing it as a nexus to serve between worlds and with any small amount of energy which you may have raised to Open this Shrine, you do not want to follow this up by dissipating it at the end! As the Shrine will serve as a permanent sacred space, each time that you enter it, energy is accumulated for use towards your purposes.

As the Shrine is also the *het neter Ast* - the Divine House (Temple) of the Goddess Herself, who presides over the work, it is She who protects the place and the practitioner from the types of things that banishings are used for. While it may take some time to adjust to the differences inherent, between a temporary and portable sacred-space and a permanently established location, the differences are important to understand, as is the recognition that each has its place and purpose and that one approach does not always remove the need for the other. An example of this would be if you were on holiday and needed to establish a temporary (or semi-permanent) ritual space; in this case at the end of the holiday, or upon moving house, a form of banishing would be used to dissipate the energy, as an ethical means of returning a space to a 'new' state and also not to subject the next tenants to spiritual forces which they have not consciously requested/agreed to access.

Once established, the Temple must be attended regularly and the basic and preliminary acts of sweeping and refreshing candles and offerings needs to be maintained. All offerings must be removed before spoiling and discarded apart from the regular rubbish; as divine offerings they are worthy of special treatment even after the spiritual force of the food/drink has been consumed. Over time, a true Temple will emerge.

4.

UR HEKA

An important part of the daily and the annual rites is the utterance of *ur heka* - 'great words of magick'. That Ast and by extension, Her Priesthood are skilled in both the utterance and the usage of these words is shown both from the praise titles with which Ast is addressed and the role of Magickian which She fulfils within the ancient legends.

One of Ast's titles is 'Mistress of Magick' and 'She who utters the divine words with the correct pronunciation of Her mouth'. In this regard, it is interesting to note that the consonant 'R', which forms the hieroglyph for the word '*ur*', is drawn in the glyph of an open mouth. The connection, both ancient and modern between the power of the word, incantation,spells and magick is well attested to. It is for these reasons that the utterance of certain spoken and sung formulae play an important role in worshipping/working with Isis and other Egyptian powers in a manner pleasing to Her and also in accordance with the ancient temple practises. What follows is the text of a Traditional Hymn to Ast, from the wall of Her primary Temple at Philae, Her Holy Place; within its words, which have been spoken and sung to Her for many thousands of years, is revealed much about this powerful Goddess' ancient identity:

"Re is in celebration
The heart exults in joy
For your heart is soft and sweet O Goddess!
Isis Queen of the World and Her son Horus
He is King upon the Throne of His Father
Governing both poles
The Seat of Geb is in Her possession
The function of Atum is in Her hand
The strength of Mentu is in Her grasp
The divinity who produces the beginning
And fills the Sky and Earth with Her perfection
This Crown who bright in Gold appears
Auguste is Her sign
Lives in the House Divine
Sovereign of the gods of the Sky
Queen of the gods of the Earth
Falcon also of gods of the Tuat
The Mistress of Bright Glory
On the Throne is Her command
It is the one Her heart desires
Who is chosen to ascend the Throne
Without violence they ascend the Palace
One call one desire to see
The honour of the country and everything whole
It is by Her order that the Temple is blessed
With the return of Her brother !
Her name is pronounced and the world is loyal to Her" (9)

Within this beautiful and evocative ancient Hymn, the primary motifs of Isis' power are proclaimed; not only is Ast "Queen of the World", as indeed She must have seemed at that late stage in Egyptian history after the Unification of Upper and Lower Egypt and the installation of the foreign Ptolemaic Pharoahs from Greece, effectively 'globalising' Her worship throughout the known world; but She is also "in possession" of awesome powers of both Creation (Atum) and

Destruction (Mentu). That Her Throne bridged the three realms of Sky, Earth and Tuat is also affirmed. An allusion to Her in the form of Het-Heru (Gk. Hathor) is also made with the praise-term "This Crown who bright in Gold appears " - a reference to Het-Heru's Horns and Disk headdress of Gold and representing the Solar forces and also in the name "Mistress of bright glory". Another interesting line shows that Ast's proper dwelling place for all time is "in the house divine", the original hieroglyphs that this was translated from on the wall of Her Temple most likely being het neter, the Egyptian title for a Temple.

Another mighty characteristic of the Goddess is that it is She and no-one else, who is solely responsible for the selection of each successive ruler and that this is not a role which may be assumed out of personal desire or lust for power. That Her praise-hymn acknowledges this, gives cause for a greater faith in the ancient Dynastic Kingship system than in today's political arena, where leaders usually exhibit no spiritual foresight and often lack even personal ethics.Whilst it is undeniable that certain Pharoahs certainly abused their privileged and unquestioned position; there were many others who strove to uphold the ancient and powerful ways of their ancestors and succeeded in establishing Egypt as a place without rival. Ast's position as Elder-sister and King-maker, a role embodied in each successive Eldest-daughter and Wife, underlines a pattern of a spiritual and loving leadership; it is also undeniable that the Throne was bestowed upon each successor as an act of love, as no-one would deny that the Goddess or Her representative could have ruled in their own right.

It is this loving attitude and example of power, in an ambience of peace, that is praised with the words that Ast always achieves what "Her heart desires...Without violence"; for She is ever the Lady who Greets the Non-Aggressor, one of Her praise-titles.

Neither should this come as a surprise - for Ast well - knows the high cost of violence, having experienced the murder of Her brother-lover, by a younger brother, who lusted after His Throne. Little wonder then, that Ast turns Her heart away from both violence and those who perpetrate such acts, particularly when acts aimed at depriving another of their rights are involved. She is ever a Lady who creates freedom and her followers should seek to act in a manner in accordance with what "Her heart desires..."

This in itself is an awesome power and one of increasing value in today's world, where it often seems that everywhere you turn, people are resorting to violence to achieve their aims, including governments and large multi-national companies. That no diminishment of power accompanies performing work "without violence" is emphasised with the acknowledgement that both the Throne is filled and Asar resurrected - "It is by her order that the temple is blessed with the return of Her brother!" - utilising precisely this non-violent force. For women, this divine precedent of magickal strength and accomplishment is a profound inspiration. There is nothing of the passive female here; Isis embodies both sovereign power and magickal skill without the martial (i.e. war-making) aspect, an aspect which seems to have been increasingly put forward as the embodiment of 'real' strength and power, usually masculine. For men, perhaps this goddess presents a challenge to long-held notions of female power, for Ast demonstrates - with devastating effectiveness -that strength and success in one's ventures lay independent of aggressive and dominating attitudes.

A simple and clear way to delineate sacred space is the utterance of ur heka. Such words of power may include formulae for both banishing and invoking,statement of intention, recitation of the names of the powers and hymns of praise and celebration. The need for all ur heka to be spoken or sung in a certain manner is shown within one traditional manner of addressing Ast: 'may thy windpipe be whole, for you never falter in the pronunciation of the divine names and your mouth never falters in the utterance of the words of power, may the North wind ever waft a sweet breeze unto thy nose O, goddess, for you are a Mistress of magick, strong and mighty are the pronunciations which you make'. Such a declaration can be preceded, or followed, with the petition: 'may I like you be a...'; or 'may my mouth not falter in the utterance of the words of power'.

That the use of music to accompany such words and hymns is appropriate, is also suggested by both the pattern of the words themselves and also the presence of musical instruments in the hands of priestesses, such as the sistrum - a sacred musical tool which symbolised the elemental powers of creation and was/is used to banish and dispel chaos.

It is of benefit to notice the different effect that speaking and singing the same words has upon yourself and also your ritual area. Another beneficial exercise is to create praise-songs and verses yourself, utilising a combination of the goddess' ancient titles and powers with your intention in harmony with these aspects. It is often in the spontaneous expression of inspiration that Isis is revealed for:

> *With a luminous veil*
> *Does She conceal*
> *The bright darkness*
> *Of Her face.* (10)

Apart from these uses, ur heka serve as a bridge between the divine, creative realm and ourselves. It is through the use of such words that we, too, may employ our human faculties, such as speech, in an elevated manner and through affirming our kinship with the powers we honour, our consciousness is exalted.

The use of such words to align human and divine is demonstrated with the following verse, which contains the titles of Ast as also used by the Egyptian Queens and priestesses in order to assert their kinship with the Goddess:

"O Isis, the Great, God's Mother
Lady of Philae
God's Wife, God's Adorer, God's Hand
God's Mother and Great Royal Spouse
Adornments of the palace
Lady and desire of the green fields
Nursling who fills the palace with her beauty
Fragrance of the palace
Mistress of Joy
Who runs her course in the Divine Palace
Rain-cloud which makes green (the fields) when it
                                                descends

Maiden, sweet of love,
Lady of Upper and Lower Egypt
Who issues orders among the divine Ennead
According to whose command one rules
Princess, great of praise
Lady of charm
Whose face loves the joy of fresh myrrh." (11)

The motifs of power described in this praise-song are in keeping with the views of Ast presented in the Hymn from Her temple at Philae previously discussed and yet, in this verse another side of the goddess is presented in addition to being one "Who issues orders among the divine Ennead " (for explanation of the Ennead, see Chapter. 1.); a fecund, loving and sensuous side to Her nature is also revealed. With words of longing is She addressed in Her aspect of Het-heru (Hathor), with words such as "beauty", "fragrance","sweet of love" and "Lady of Charm", it becomes clear that Ast embodies a range of qualities, some which are more 'masculine' - to do with 'orders', 'commands' and 'rulership'; others which are wholly 'feminine'. It is necessary for the goddess to change forms, shifting between a more introvert and extrovert phase; between Her aspects as Ast and Het-heru for example, in order to transmit the power of the Throne to Earth.

This view of the goddess transcends notions of duality, for She exhibits a wholeness, a unity in Herself. It is because of this and because of Her 'knowledge of the words of power', that Ast is able to accomplish not only the resurrection of Asar, but also and more potently, the creation and birth of Heru (Horus) unaided. It is also important to remember that actual women ceremonially represented the goddess in Her many aspects and that these women also literally ruled Egypt, as sister and wife of the Pharoah and also as the highest priestesses in the land. By keeping this in mind, you also begin to understand the ideal of female power which the Egyptians both revered and aspired to embody in their religious and secular cultures.

It is to this lofty aspect that She is addressed in another of the ancient cult chants of Ast in Her form of Het-heru:

"*O perfect, O lightness, O great*
O Great Magician
O Mistress Light
O Gold of Gods!

The King of the South and the North, Pharaoh
He salutes you with respect
You are the Key of Life !
O Gold of Gods
He salutes you with respect
Hail Key of Life !" [12]

That Pharoah himself addressed the Goddess in such terms is revealing; as both the mother of the sun and the sun itself, the sphere of such profound importance within the Egyptian

82

religion, Het-heru was indeed the "Key of Life". This allusion to the Goddess is doubly interesting, for it also puns on the sacred symbol of the Ankh, which itself is referred to in this same manner and is a symbol which combines the forces of life in a creative union.

The Cult of Hathor was widely renowned for its fecund rites, involving feasting, consumption of large quantities of ritual beer and wine and also sexual rites. The high point of Het-heru's Ritual Calendar at Her primary Temple at Denderah involved the transportation of the sacred Hawk from Heru' (Horus') Temple at nearby Edfu, to enable union with the Goddess' Hawk at Denderah. This of course was a rite of supreme symbolic importance and one which was replicated by the Pharoah (as the 'Hawk Horus') and the highest Priestess of the Goddess annually to ensure both the continued well-being of both the land and Pharoah's house. The necessity of Pharoah to revere this source and to "salute...with respect" also emphasises the Goddess as the source of power of the Throne.

The bountiful and joyous side of Ast's religion was balanced with a solemn and mournful side surrounding the loss of Her lover-brother Asar (Osiris) and it is this aspect which is usually referred to as the Veiled or Mourning Isis:

> " 'I am thy sister Isis, the desire of thine heart,
> yearning after thy love whilst thou art far away;
> I flood the land with tears today.
>
> I am a woman beneficial to her brother,
> Thy wife, thy sister, by thine own mother,
> Come thou to me quickly,
> Since I desire to see thy face
> After not having seen thy face...
> My heart is hot at thy wrongful separation;
> I yearn for thy love toward me,

Come ! Be not alone ! Be not far off !...
I hid me in the bulrushes to conceal
Thy son in order to avenge thee,
And it is not fitting for thy flesh...
Hot are the hearts of myriads of persons,
Great sorrow is amongst the Gods." (13)

Of all the praise-songs of Ast, this one stands out in its ability to convey a sense of the immense love the Goddess has for Osiris and also the emptiness with which She felt after His murder. Alluded to in this verse are several important ritual dates of Ast's Temple; including the Inundation season - "I flood the land with tears today ", Ast's magickal conception of Heru following Asar's death - "Come thou quickly to me.." and Her subsequent protection of the Child, "I hid me in the bulrushes to conceal thy son", until he was old enough "to avenge" His father. Her devotion to duty is such that She, a Queen did not feel it beneath Her to hide amidst the tall rushes of the Delta region in order to ensure the protection of the young heir to the Throne. In this She was aided, particularly by the Goddess Neith and Lord Tehuti (Thoth). It is within these expressions that the passion of the Goddess emerges and also Her magickal potency and loyalty. Little wonder that Isis became renowned as the model wife and mother and that She was beloved of the Gods is also confirmed by the verse that "Great sorrow is amongst the Gods", as they partake with Her in mourning the loss of the rightful King. When enacted in ritual, a Priestess taking this role of the Goddess will undoubtedly 'feel ' the Goddess' sorrow. (see chapter.7)

At formal times of celebration, it is useful to have a ritual declaration that enunciates the power of Ast and provides a means of conveying a sense of the responsibility that devotees of Her Temple are required to exhibit:

Behold the Goddess Isis
She who lived in the body of a woman
A Mistress of Magick
Who has knowledge of the
Words of power

Her heart turned away in disgust
From the millions of men
She chose for herself the
Millions of the Gods
Esteeming more highly the
Millions of the spirits

She came with Her words of Power
In Her mouth is the breath of life
Now when She stringeth together Words
Diseases are destroyed and
Those whose throats are stopped up
Are made to live
All poisons flow out and
She makes the Eye of Horus
Come forth from the God and
Shine outside His mouth
She blesses those who tread Her path
Reminding us of Her benevolence Isis says:
'I have come to be a protector of thee
I waft unto thee air for thy nostrils
And the North wind from the God Tem
Flows unto thy nose
I have made whole thy windpipe
I make thee to live like a god
Thy enemies fall under thy feet
I have made thy word to be True before Nut
And thou art mighty before the Gods'
She does protect those of her Temple
Repulsing all fiends
Turning away all calamities

Beneficent in Word and Command is Ast
Her tongue is Perfect
It has never halted a word
She utters all spells with the
Magickal power of Her mouth
For She is a Mistress of Magick
The advocate of Her Brother. (14)

In addition to the use of ur heka in the form of praise songs during ritual, there are other words which are frequently used within Ast's Temple that contain particular aspects of power; what follows is a rite which may be used to Open the Shrine of the Goddess upon awaking - immediately after bathing and preceding any other of the day's activities, the practitioner enters the Shrine, or ritual area used which contains Ast's image (papyrus, statue) and performs the following:

Ritual to Open the Shrine

Facing East: Salute the altar and say out loud *Hail Ast* (or, Isis).

Raising your dominant arm and hand, palm facing the altar say your name.

Close your eyes and visualise a sphere of immense light and power above.

Raising your dominant arm and hand. Draw that light down to the crown of your head as you vibrate the word tua, touch your brow and continue to draw the light down in a bright and clear shaft to your heart and vibrate *shen*, continue to draw the light down to you genital area and vibrate *taui* bless your right shoulder and vibrate *necht*, then pull the light across your chest and vibrate *cheser*; draw the light down to your genital area again, tracing a triangular pattern; then bring both hands up to heart level and joining your palms vibrate the words *uba maa, aha en hay*; complete this by repeating the *tua - shen -* taui vibrations.

Draw in a deep breath, trace a banishing Ankh in the East, then envisage Ast's Throne ideogram and vibrate her divine name Ast. Face North, do as before, tracing the banishing Ankh to the North, then envisage the Cobra ideogram and vibrate the divine name Neb-t seker. Face West, do as before, tracing the banishing Ankh to the West and envision the Basket within the Palace ideogram and vibrate the divine name *Neb-t het*. Face South, do as before and envision the Hawk within the Palace ideogram and vibrate the divine name *Het-heru*. This effectively surrounds the Shrine with the protective influence of these four Goddesses. Stand facing your altar again and vibrate (and visualise): to the East: Heru; to the West Asar; to the South Anpu; to the North Tehuti. This balances the energy of the Shrine and invokes the blessing of four god-forms, bringing the energy of an eightfold divine force to the Shrine

Kneel before your altar,seated upon your feet assuming the position of supplication and reverence; raise both hands to shoulder height, pushing the palms outwards towards the Goddess and vibrate *tua neter Ast* four times (i.e. once for each of the cardinal directions, as you do this immense light may become apparent around the Goddess' image.

Light altar candles and any incense at this point. The incense may then be raised in offering towards the altar and utilised to encircle the Goddess. Here follows the recitation, or singing of a praise-song and the making of *hetepu neter* (see following chapter for suggestions), as well as any petitions which you might have/requests for aid.

Then stand, slightly back from the altar (centre of the room if the altar is in the East) and raising either your dominant arm and hand, or a ritual tool of choice (e.g. a Lotus Wand or Sceptre), say aloud:

Awake great Queen, Awake   (trace Ankh around the altar)

Arise Great Queen in Strength   (trace the Tjed symbol)

May thy arising and awakening

Be with the peaceful power you possess. (trace Uas symbol)

Take one step towards the altar and raise your dominant arm and hand and taking a deep breath inwards point to the centre of the wall immediately above and behind the altar, raising the Wand begin to formulate a circle with three rays of light descending from it that also have arrow-like barbs on each shaft and vibrate aakhuti once for each of three times that you trace this symbol and then bringing both feet together and opening your arms wide say:

I am a Being of Light

In my shining forth is there strength

May my Light shine forth to illumine the path ahead

May my Light shine forth to guide and bless my life.

With this sequence, the Shrine is effectively awakened and you have established a beneficient divine ambience to accompany you throughout the day.

A Note on this Ritual
The ancient pattern of the power of Creation within the Egyptian system takes as an underlying reference to the following combinations -

The Ennead
The Ogdoad
The duality of Male-Female
The duality of Light-Dark
The generations of Father-Son (an Elder and Younger
    male aspect)
The generations of Mother-Daughter (an Elder and
    Younger female aspect)

All of these patterns contain within themselves the prerequisite of balanced force which enables Creation and Renewal to take place and as evidenced within the many Creation Legends, all of these patterns are potent and effective. This is one of the most important points and keys, for these Divine patterns show forth the ways by which each one, whether male or female; whether working together or alone, may just as effectively create in their lives. These patterns also offer Divine precedents for the magickal potency of practitioners whose gender and sexuality does not encompass a male-female polarity.

Whether one pattern or the other is more personally applicable should not prevent awareness of the variety of means by which both Creation and Renewal may take place within Egyptian Rites and this must also be stated: that as neither pattern was superior or inferior to these ancients, neither should they be to us. All things have their appropriate place within the cosmos. To some practitioners this may be an immense relief and awakening, for ancient patterns of magickal potency and wholeness which embrace all genders and possible combinations, without bias, have not been loudly proclaimed. To others, comfortable with the familiar patterns, this information may arouse scepticism, or perhaps, unfortunately, hostility; but if this is the case, please consider why it makes you feel this way and the manner in which the ancient world-view was an encompassing whole, a place in which nothing is diminished through the acknowledgement of the power of the other - this also applies personally. It is also true that we individually have the responsibility to grow to a wholeness magickally and to allow others to do the same - regardless of our personal preference (this works both ways, whether you are in a minority or in the majority). Leaving matters such as this unspoken has created and only continues to perpetuate an atmosphere of denial and suppression, which apart from being unhealthy, ultimately misrepresents the ancient Egyptian understanding of the neter.

It is recommended that a personal investigation and deep study of ancient Egyptian Creation Legends be undertaken - that every person who aspires to practise an Egyptian magickal philosophy may make up their own mind as to the role what is discovered should play in your overall perception and work with these realms.

It will also be noted that by the practitioner entering the Shrine and Opening, it in this way, Invoking Four Goddesses and Four Gods, that a pattern of Nine (an Ennead) is represented, or One accompanied by the Eight (an Ogdoad).

The portion of Light created by the Eight in combination with the Nine is so potent, that when employed by Tehuti, the Five Children of Nut and Geb were able to be born. The Nine (Ennead) multiplied by the Eight (Ogdoad) gives Seventy - Two; or one-fifth of the Three-hundred and Sixty which equals both time and traces the annual movement of light. This has important underlying symbolic references for our work and provides a key pattern which provides an ancient framework for all types of Creation.

5.

Hetepu Neter

Within the region of the Tuat, those who were deemed to be of good character were divided into two groups; the *Maatiut* and the *Hetepiut*. The *Maatiut*, as the *Maat* section of the name implies, were the Speakers of Truth, who offered the Hymns of Praise and the prescribed Litanies of the gods. The *Hetepuit* (*Het*, i.e. house, temple), on the other hand, were in charge of making the daily offerings. As is the case with many other details of the *Tuat* Journey, a parallel exists with the realm of Earth, in this case, with those within the Temple responsible for these ceremonial tasks. The clear distinction of these roles reveals the importance with which they were regarded, for the gods and goddesses were seen to be dependent upon the priestly class/devotees for their daily sustenance and maintenance and in return for this devotion and care, they aided in turn.

Hetepu Neter, or 'divine offerings of the Temple'; always played a prominent part in rites and are equally important for practitioners today. The types of offerings in common usage are extensive and well-documented, both in written records and in mural paintings and ranged from full banquets provided by the Highest Priest (Pharoah) or his designated substitute; to simpler offerings of bread and beer accompanied by the appropriate *Ur Heka* and incense. Flowers also played an important role in the offerings, both upon the altar before the goddess and also in the hair and hands of the priestesses.

Where availability of produce was limited and in later times, paintings upon the walls of the Temples and pyramids were used as a substitute for the 'real thing' and were deemed to be awakened and rendered useable, again by the appropriate words of power. The applications for this within a modern setting - such as for the decoration of a shrine,or even a book are apparent.Here follow a selection of Traditional offerings and the aspect of Isis to which they are best suited:

Hetepu Neter	Aspect
Bread, cake	Staple of life - all aspects.
Dates	Fruit of Tree of Life - all aspects.
Honey	Het-heru; Ast-Maat.
Egg	Neb-t seker; Uadjit (Ur-aeus); Serpent "tch".
Pomegranate	Sekhmet; Red Queen aspects.
Raisins	Het-heru; all aspects.
Melon	All aspects.
Coconut	Purification.
Lotus	Plant of Lower Egypt; Union.
Papyrus	Plant symbol of Upper Egypt;Scribe.
Palm Leaf	Symbol of victory; Initiation.
Rose/rosewater	Het-heru; Red Queen aspects;Silence.
Rainwater	Purification; also linked to Ast-sept.
Beer	All aspects.
Pomegranate beer	Sekhmet; some rites of Het-heru.
Black wine	Ast; Binah.
White wine	Ast; stellar.
Milk	Ast en mut neter (Divine Mother); Het-heru.
Natron	Purification; all aspects.
Myrrh	Black Queen; Veiled goddess; Purification.
Olibanum	Consecration; Het-heru; Invocation.
Various thighs of meat, geese	Annual rites.

The feeding of the Goddess/Gods is of vital importance within the context of both the daily and the yearly rites and provides the practitioner with a means of both giving something back (energy exchange) and as a means of devotional in its own right. It is important to make hetepu neter on a regular basis and to make especial offerings on those high celebrations of the annual cycle, such as the Lychapsia and Ast's Birthday, or when it is necessary to give thanks for work accomplished, or blessings received. At such times, it is appropriate to provide a sumptuous banquet of foods and drink. The making of such offerings creates and maintains a beneficient astral ambience within the shrine.

Aligned to this work is the recognition, that just as certain offerings are aligned to particular aspects of Ast more so than others, so also, are they more suitable to particular days of the week. Utilising the seven-fold division of the week familiar today, we will establish an awareness of which planetary energies hetepu neter are aligned to and utilising this as a basis, it is suggested that alternative offerings be selected based upon local seasonal availability wherever the rites are performed. The planet which 'rules' each day is shown in brackets following the day.

MONDAY	(Moon):	Lotus, Melon, Coconut, Milk, White Wine,
TUESDAY	(Mars):	Pomegranate,Pomegranate Beer,
WEDNESDAY	(Mercury):	Papyrus,
THURSDAY	(Jupiter):	Lotus and Papyrus,
FRIDAY	(Venus):	Rose/Rosewater,Palm Leaf,Bread,Cake,Dates,
SATURDAY	(Saturn):	Myrrh,Black Wine,Natron,
SUNDAY	(Sun):	Honey, Raisins, Olibanum, Egg, Various Thighs of Meat, Geese,

Whilst some of these items are readily available worldwide, others present a difficulty due to the specific climate in which they flourish. It becomes necessary then for an understanding of the underlying reasoning behind the offerings, to enable a suitable substitution to be made. Behind hetepu neter are both legends and local custom supporting use. An example of this is the use of Lotus and Papyrus as plants both suited to individual days of the week and also combined on another. As the plant emblems of Upper (Lotus) and Lower (Papyrus) Egypt, they are well suited to be combined as an offering on Thursday a day whose symbolism includes rulership and the public sphere. On their individual days, Papyrus, a plant of scribes, is suited to Mercurial Wednesday, a day of 'words of power' both written and spoken; whilst the water-grown Lotus is a fitting plant to be offered on the Lunar day (Monday).

There are some excellent modern alternatives for these traditional offerings whilst still maintaining precise planetary sympathy; for example, for 'Black Wine', one of Saturday's selections, a deep black elderberry liquor (Black Sambucca) is a perfect choice, as it combines the Saturnian Elderberry in a deeply dark spirit, very evocative of Binah (Ast as Sovereign Queen) when it is in a sacred vessel.

An alternative for Lotus, a plant which is only readily available in the hottest Summer months (and may be difficult to obtain in colder countries) are the flowers of the White Lily family (eg Madagascan Lily, Queen of the Night,Trumpet Lily); or for a Blue Lotus substitute, Blue Iris is an alternative available in colder climates. Lotus may also be obtained in a seed form for consumption, many Oriental food markets stock Lotus flowers and seeds as they are utilised in a wide range of cooked dish.

There are other *hetepu neter* not so easily substituted, for example, pomegranate - which has a complex lore behind it pertaining to Sekhmet (the Lioness-headed warrior form of Het-heru). It is said that She became so enraged in battle, slaughtering mankind, that Ra himself feared that all would perish. It was he who designed the 'trick' of placing numerous jugs of beer coloured with pomegranate juice, to imitate blood, upon the battlefield and when the Goddess next arrived, thirstily She drank of the liquid and becoming drunk, She fell asleep. To this day Priestesses of the Solar aspect consume this red fluid in Her honour; ritual drunkenness also being a feature of the worship of Het-heru (Hathor), the Goddess of bounteous beauty and joy. It is because of this importance that a substitution would be difficult and also because of the precious fluid (i.e. blood) which it is intended to represent. Pomegranate has other rich associations which may be revealed through meditation upon the open ripened fruit.

Forms of *hetepu neter* have always encompassed both the offering of the sweet and the salt;this means that whilst some offerings would 'appeal' to the modern practitioner, such as cake and honey, other aspects may be difficult to minds born in cities where all food comes neatly wrapped in plastic. The making of hetepu neter to the Red Queen is an area which may be dealt with on both the symbolic and other levels and is beyond the scope of this chapter.

It is an undeniable fact of history, that offerings of flesh, sacramentally slaughtered, including the pouring of blood from captured enemies at the base of the altar, has always been part of the Temple Tradition. Though these may seem repugnant today, the underlying importance of the offering of the precious life essence - in both a symbolic and literal form - to the source of life is still valid. As in the ancient Temple, the finest specimens are always selected for consumption and in one way, the slaughtering of the animals within the Temple domain ensured that only the unblemished and the freshest produce was presented upon the altar. It is obvious why such care would be taken, remembering also that these were days long before refrigeration. Utilising the principle that a part of a thing may stand for the whole and with meditation, ways of approaching this aspect with suitable offerings may present themselves.

No matter which aspect of Ast, or which day of the week the offerings are made, elements which should be included are: food/drink traditionally favoured as auspicious and also the practitioner should add to the list food/drink that they feel is appropriate, as well as pure water, incense and candles. All offerings should be arranged in a meticulous fashion, with the choicest portions being arranged upon a platter which is then offered to Ast and placed upon Her altar. This is then left upon the altar for different time periods depending upon the reason for the offering; however in the case of a petition that will take longer than three days, the offering must be regularly replenished and in all cases, it must be removed while fresh. NEVER allow an offering to deteriorate or spoil in the presence of the divine; not only an obvious insult and showing a careless attitude, but one which will disrupt the energy of the shrine and require a purificatory rite and further offerings to be made.

Here follow some incense blends,including modern forms of the extremely sacred Khyphi and which may be utilised as part of the hetepu neter for all rites of invocation:

Ast Sep-t (Sirius Blend)	Khyphi #1 (Summer)	Khyphi #2 (Winter)
Vervain leaves	Lemon Grass	Lemon Grass
Benzoin	Ginger	Vervain
Star Anise	Frankincense	Olibanum Resinoid
Frankincense (optional)	Orris Root	Benzoin
	Patchouli	Wind
	Raisins	Raisins
	Wind	Honey
	Honey	

With the ingredients for Khyphi #1,#2, it is important that a large quantity of fresh lemon grass is used, preferably grown by the practitioner and picked with an appropriate thanksgiving just prior to use. The lemon grass is pounded and ground thoroughly, in a mortar and pestle, as is the ginger in the first version and to these moist ingredients are added to the raisins and all dry ingredients, also all pounded and ground together. Then add a little honey to moisten the mixture further and enable th resultant fragrant pulp to be rolled into small round balls, symbolic of the Solar Disc which Khephera rolls across the sky. The wind, an important ingredient in both blends, is symbolic of several things, including the Sky wherein the Sun arises, the North Wind - most favoured for its sweet and refreshing breezes in the Nile Valley and the ur heka uttered during the incense' making. These balls are then placed upon a tray and left to dry for between three and seven days, before either use or storage; if stored before dry, the incense will most likely go a little moldy on the surface. Best results are obtained by breaking a disk open before placing face down upon a lighted charcoal. the resultant smoke and lingering odour is truly evocative of the ancient and glorious temples.

The use of oil is also important within rites of offering and is aligned to the element of Spirit (aethyr, akasha). Oil is used to anoint things - both people, ritual objects, candles and certain food offerings (e.g. eggs). Scented oils may be made to align to particular aspects of the Goddess' service; a useful basic oil blend follows:

Temple Oil:
Pure Oil (Base of Olive or Apricot kernel is suggested)
Rose
Frankincense
Honey

Lunar Oil	Solar Oil	Stellar Oil
Pure Oil Base	Pure Oil Base	Pure Oil Base
Lotus	Lemon	Ameranthus
Wormwood	Ginger	Star Anise/Aniseed
	Olibanum	Vervain
	Honey	

It is suggested that these oils be made on the appropriate day of the week and at a suitable time to maximise their potency (e.g. a Full Moon on a Monday for the Lunar blend or the hour of the Moon on a Monday and for the solar blend, Midday Sunday). The Stellar Oil is best made on the first day of the New Moon, when there is still no moon visible in the sky and at the time of star-rise.

A further feature of hetepu neter and one which combines the devotional attitude of making an offering, with artistic skill and ur heka; is in the performance of music and dance within the Temple to accompany the feasts at the end of certain rituals. That music and dance were a formal part of the ancient Temple traditions, is evident through both the accounts of the festivals held by these Temples and also repeated references to the Goddess' 'Dancing Maidens' - particularly featured amongst the Temple attendants of Het-heru. Undoubtedly, this was a specialised area and formed by a distinct sacred class of younger Priestesses and devotees of the Goddess, who possessed the requisite grace and agility for entertaining Her.

This is an area which is worthy of reinstating within the modern service of both Ast and other Egyptian deities. Whilst the actual details of what type of dances were performed has not come down to us through an oral / performance tradition, like many other cultures, it is possible to reconstruct an overall concept of what is suitable for Temple dances from both a study of tomb paintings,sculptures and also from the types of music and dance still performed by Egyptian, Middle-Eastern and African peoples.

Certain points become apparent from researching the above: that small drums, flutes, tambourines, bells, whistles, hand-clapping, the shaking of sistra, singing, reciting of rhythmic verses and the spontaneous calling out of praise-names of the Goddess and other joyous rhythm; all form an appropriate basis upon which to recreate the ancient Temple sounds. As for dances, one possible starting point, is in combining a series of ritual postures to music and gradually building up the pace; if performed gracefully the external appearance accords with that of other spiritual-physical disciplines e.g Tai Chi and undoubtedly would have a revitalising effect upon the body.

Another type of dance suited to use within the Temple is undoubtedly the Middle Eastern and Egyptian 'belly dancing', which has a long and venerable history of use amongst women as a form of entertainment - each hand gesture and body contouring meaning a particular thing, especially connected to the desert regions. It is unfortunate, that this, like many other aspects which once were sacred, have become disinherited of their origins.

The performance of music and dance within the Temple is an area sorely neglected and in need of much work to restore it to its rightful place amongst the Egyptian rites. It is encouraged, that anyone with the requisite skill, or interest, look into this area and also those naturally talented both in dance and music may feel inspired to recreate these Temple arts and share them with a wider audience.

Times within the Annual Ritual Cycle particularly suited to this type of offering are: Ast's Birthday; Egyptian New Year; the Harvest and Setting Forth to Sea Festival; Rites of Het - heru and Bast in general as these are essentially all rites of life and joy - included in this would be rituals performed to celebrate the birth of a new child, marriage and other sacred unions. Times when this celebratory offering are not appropriate include: the Veiling of the Goddess and during Her Mourning Phase and funerary rites in general.

It is hoped that this section will encourage participants in the living mysteries of Egypt to be inspired to assist in rebuilding the ancient Temple to a new glory in modern times and one in which all skills and talents may be brought into use within the blessed domain of the eternal neter.

6.

Lighting the Lamps

In Pre-Dynastic times the worship of the Cobra as the pre-
eminent Clan Totem of the North in the form of the
primordial self-Creatrix Goddess Neith of Sais, set in place
the pattern of power of one half of the Sovereign emblems,
which in Dynastic times became revered as the Two Ladies, or
the two Mistresses, Uadjet (Uraeus) and Nekhbet; who
together represented the powers of Life and Death which the
Pharoah required to rule. In earlier days, the Vulture Goddess
Nekhbet was also revered as the Clan Totem of Nekhen in the
South. For centuries these two were the tutelary Goddesses of
the powers of birth, death and re-birth in their respective
lands;both protecting mothers-to -be and nursing the dead
back to a new life. It is little wonder that long after the Clans
were assimilated into the highly organised way of life of the
forty-two Nomes, or provinces of Egypt; that their worship
would continue at an intensified and exalted level as the
Mistresses responsible for the life and well-being of the
Pharoah himself.

It is of great importance to understanding the powers
contained within the Sovereign emblems to acknowledge that
they were and are both Goddesses. Some confusion in later
times surrounding the gender of the Cobra, Uraeus as male,
needs to be replaced with the accurate understanding that, in
ancient Egyptian times, the Cobra hieroglyph was the
determinative sign used interchangeably to denote a Goddess,

Priestess,or a Woman and was not used in a masculine sense; a God, Priest, or a Man being represented by a Hawk. The gender of the Cobra, being female, holds importance also when you consider that the inheritance of the Throne came through the Eldest daughter and passed to Her brother-lover. Women were also known to have ruled as Pharoah - acknowledged as a female Horus; an example of this is Hatshesput. In all other cases in Dynastic times, it was the power of the great ancestress-Goddess, in the form of the Cobra or the Vulture, which was re-born in the form of the eldest daughter and through marriage, became the tutelary protectress of the King. In this context, it is also worth spending some time meditating the high role and true position which the Queenly-sister held and also the consequences of displeasing the Goddess-incarnate. All of this contains references to the original form of secular-sacred power which was passed through the rite of hierogamos.

So it comes to pass that one of the lesser-known ritual dates of the ancient calendar, June 24th, the Lighting of the Lamps, is paradoxically also one of its most important. On this night, in a solemn and silent ceremony, Priestesses make their way into the Temples of Neith in Sais and of Ast in Philae. Neith, the ancestress of Uadjet embodies the powers of the North, whilst Ast in Her role as the Vulture Queen embodies the powers of the South. Together, these Two Ladies contain the source powers of life and death that maintain the fecundity and welfare of the land in perpetuity.

Cogent symbols adorning the Temples on this night are their sacred plant emblems the papyrus and the lotus. Everything on this occasion is focused upon the symbolic renewal of the ages-old Unification of Upper and Lower Egypt. At a designated time, lamps are lit simultaneously in both Temples, representing the Two Ladies and the Two Lands in a peaceful union. Whilst this is a silent and solemn ceremony, it is in its profound simplicity that is its strength. For the

Lamps that are lit at this time represent the spiritual and intellectual light of the Goddesses themselves, ever-present in the night-sky in their stellar abodes.

It is the interconnection between the source of ancestral power, the stars and the representation of that power in the form of lamplight, that we begin to perceive this annual rite as a means by which the star/light of both Neith and Ast was brought within the inner sanctuaries simultaneously in a way which would not have been possible otherwise except through some rare and auspicious occurrence celestially, such as if their two stars were to rise simultaneously and the star-light naturally penetrate the shrines. Such risings have been recorded in Egyptian religion, such as the rising of Ast's star Sep-t (Sirius) and the Sun, as recorded on the Denderah Zodiac. But in the absence of such a celestial occurrence, what better way to represent it through rite of sympathetic magick, than through this rite of Lighting the Lamps? In another manner, Ast and Neith are sister-goddesses, both born of the same star, Sep-t; thus the Lighting of the Lamps at this time pre-figures the rising of that star.

The annual timing of this rite is of great importance: falling as it does immediately after the shortest day of the year, Summer Solstice, a time of immense heat and abundant light; this is a time in the Annual Ritual Cycle when sky and stellar rites are the focus of the Temple. There is this ceremony of lights symbolising Unification and nine days later, on July 3rd the commencement of the 'Dog-Days', the hottest days of Summer heralded by the rising of Sep-t is honoured. Interestingly, the rising of Sep-t (Sirius) is noted not once, but three times in the calendar; twice during the season of Shomu (or, Summer): at July 3rd, August 12th - the beginning of the Lychnapsia, or Lights of Isis festival and again as the First Day of the Inundation, the first season of the calendar, Akhe - it is on this latter day that each Pharoah ascended the Throne.

The reason behind highlighting this sequence is to emphasise that this entire portion of the ritual year and the old calendar, is focussed upon light and fire and the elements of air (realm of the celestial light bodies) and fire.In this connection, the Cobra Neith, is a fiery Goddess; whilst the Vulture Ast, is a Goddess of air. In these forms, both Cobra and Vulture were anciently revered as being capable of self-creation, that is, of parthenogenesis. The belief in this aspect of the Goddesses has persisted down to modern times and references to the Vulture as generating itself with a spiral flight in the air may be found scattered throughout magickal texts and are based upon the vulture's habit, in nature, of riding the fast and upward-moving heated air currents.

So returning to the Temple and the Lighting of the Lamps, it can be seen how the outward action, whilst still and simple, is in reality representative of much more. Each flame partakes of the nature of both its Mothers, in that the fire burns through the agency of air; the solitary lamp-light is thus profoundly suited to being emblematic of the Union of the Two Lands, as it contains within itself the Union of the Two Ladies elementally.

As the flames burn on this sacred night, within the Sister Temples Of Neith and Ast, devotees may choose to keep an all-night vigil, watching and scrying the flames. Alternatively, this would be a highly auspicious night to seek a dream oracle through embarking on an Incubation Sleep before the Shrine.Whatever is done, the lights lit on this night will continue to illumine the work of both Lands in a blessed unity for the rest of the year.

A further meditation may be made upon the nature of the Two Ladies' power through the Crowns upon which they sit. The Red Crown of the North and the White Crown of the South and the Union of the Two Lands which they represent, may also be interpreted in alchemical terms. In this form, the Red

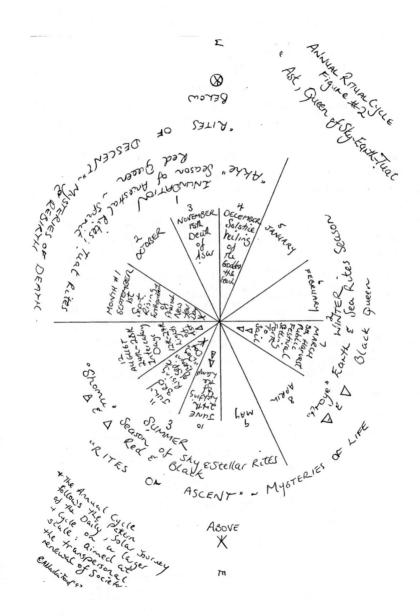

ANNUAL RITUAL CYCLE
Figure #2
Ast, Queen of Sky-Earth-Tuat

"RITES OF DESCENT" ~ MYSTERIES OF DEATH.

REBIRTH-DEATH.

INUNDATION Season of Ancestral Rites; Spirit-Tuat Rites
"Akhe" Red Queen

Σ

⊗ BELOW

1 NOVEMBER 15th Death of Asar

3

4 DECEMBER Solstice Veiling of the Goddess the Search

5 JANUARY

2 OCTOBER

MONTH #1 1st SEPTEMBER Sept. Rising New

6 FEBRUARY

7 MARCH Six Harvest Public Festival Rites; Soil

WINTER & Sea Rites Season

Black Queen

8 April

9 May

10 JUNE 24th Rising 3rd

11 JULY

12 AUGUST 25th 24th-24th Intercalary Days

"Eye" Earth △ 3

△ 2 MYSTERIES OF LIFE

"Shems" △ SUMMER Season of Sky Estellar Rites
Red & Black

"RITES OF ASCENT" ~ MYSTERIES OF LIFE

+ The Annual Cycle follows the pattern of the Daily , Solar Journey + Cycle on a larger scale: Aimed at the transpersonal renewal of Society.

@Alladirford '97

ABOVE
X

m

Crown (Cobra) is also representative of the Red Tincture and Sol, whilst the White Crown (Vulture) is also representative of the White Tincture and Luna. It is in the marriage or union of these two powers that the great androgyne figure arises and the combined Red and White Crown, these khemti [22], worn by Pharoahs after the Unification, can be seen as representative of this state. The Egyptian name of this double Crown is revealing, as it is formed of the word for great and vital force,sekhem. 'Vital force' implies being filled with an abundance of those life-giving qualities, power and energy associated with being in a state of optimum health, beneath divine blessing and able to dynamically project that energy both within and without.

'Sekhem' can also be experienced by us today as an abundance of life-force and light circulating within and through disciplines which focus upon the circulation of this life-force (e.g. Tai Chi,Yoga, Ritual). In all cultures has this 'vital force' been honoured; whether termed chi, prana, mana,or any other thing, it has always been acknowledged as the fundamental internal motivating energy of life. So, too, with the Egyptian view of both sekhem and the Crown which exemplified the highest exaltation of its force. With this in mind, the flame kindled on this night may also be lit within the shrine or body of the devotee.

7.

Annual Cycles of Renewal

1. The Lychnapsia

The lights blaze brightly within Ast's temple on each of the final twelve days of the ancient Egyptian Calendar, beginning on our August 12th each year and continuing until the 24th of the month. During this closing part of the Calendar, the emphasis is upon seeking and finding, this is understandable in terms of the imminent ending of one year and the anticipation of th beginning of another. The lights lit within the Shrine herald the approaching return of the divine ancestors of the Land, in the form of the re-born Asar, the Sun returned in the form of the son, the Pharoah and also the lights typify the the Rise of the star Sep-t, also closely aligned to the symbolism of the Pharoah's Enthronement.

The length of the Lychnapsia is highly significant: these final twelve days of the year also personify the twelve months of the calendar just experienced; the twelve zodiacal constell- ations which the Sun must pass through on His way to re- birth; the twelve Hours of the Night over which the Lights hold vigil and through which the Sun must also Journey to achieve daily re-birth within the ancestral regions of the Tuat, with His Light hidden from conscious view and finally the the twelve gates which must be passed within the Tuat (in one form) to reach the place where Sunrise occurs. Ast's Temple is illuminated with lights representing Time and Space: the year now passing and the celestial lights which oversee its movement: in this manner they serve as 'midwife' to the New Year - for they overlight and guide the passage of the new Sun and Star-rise through the Hours of the Night. the Lights of the Lychnapsia symbolise all these things and through the conscious lighting of their flames, enables the Temple to connect with these patterns.

It is because this is a time which represents the commemoration and remembrance of the sudden disappearance of the light, of the beloved ruler of Egypt, Asar who now takes a chthonic form, that this ritual cycle is called the Lights of Isis; it is She who lovingly, loyally and with great distress searches the Land for Her brother and does not rest until She is reunited with Him. In reliving the mourning of Her Veiled phase at Winter Solstice, its searching and finding leads to a renewed outpouring of tears - the annual rainy season- which in turn floods the Nile (Asar in another form); in this way they are truly reunited and eternally renewed. It is this feeling of renewal which accompanies the closing of the year and as the days of the Lychnapsia draw to a close, this feeling increases. With the Five Intercalary Days which follow, when the temple is void of Light, the Birth of the Five Children of Nut and Geb fulfils the anticipation of the Return.

KEYWORDS: Endings, new beginnings, anticipation, seeking, finding, loss, gain, grief, joy, peace, contemplation, rising, celebration, contentment, renewal.

GODFORMS: Ast, Anpu,Tehuti, Nut, Geb, Asar (& Elder Heru,Set, Neb-t het), Het-Heru,Sep-t.

From the 12th-24th August, the emphasis in the Temple is upon readiness and clarity of mind - the God must be found and there is little time to accomplish this! Whilst the Lychnapsia encompasses twelve whole days, it is in the evenings that the Temple comes alive and during which hours, the Seeking takes place. It is in the act of Lighting the candles that the Inner power of the Lychnapsia becomes activated: at this time dreams should be watched closely, for we link our subconscious mind with the Shrine by consciously lighting the flames and dreams form one means of connection with the Journey and activity of the Light, both within the regions of the Tuat and the celestial realms. The Lighting of the Lights each day symbolises the preparedness of the Temple for the imminent return of the ancestral ruler of the Land.

This also reminds us that this festival falls during the Dog-Days of the year - the earliest Rise of Sep-t being reckoned to have occurred on July 3rd, it is on August 15th that its presence in the sky is fully established, just prior to the 'Official' Rise of Sep-t, heralding New Year's Day.

The choice of colour for candles throughout these twelve nights is White; however this is not meant as a 'virginal white', but rather the stellar white luminescence which so brightly veils Ast's potent form. A minimum of two new white candles for each night is required (24 in total). Complementing this, Star Anise is used whole upon charcoal as the primary (or sole) incense throughout this time and symbolises the star Sep-t (Sirius).

Significantly, the completion of the Calendar is accomplished through the Lychhnapsia period of twelve day/nights plus the subsequent Intercalary period of five days - a total of seventeen days leading to the Rise of Sep-t in all. It forms a moot point whether the significances surrounding this time and the Rise of Sep-t which follows, provides the ancient forerunner and pattern, as well as providing additional insights into the numerological and other basis enshrouded within The Star, Atu #17 of the Major Arcanum of Tarot...

It is because the Shrine has been so filled with light during these days that the second part of this festival - the Intercalary Days - are all the more keenly felt. During these final five days of the year, days which belong neither to the old or the new, but were 'inserted' into the year through the Wisdom of Lord Tehuti, who played draughts with the Moon and won a 72nd portion of its light to enable the Children of earth (Geb) and Sky (Nut) to come forth. In symbol that the Divine Children are not yet born, the Temple remains in darkness for these days; as the Lights of the previous days have acted as sentinels, keeping vigil awaiting the return (birth) of these Ones; so now the dark implies the night-sky womb-space from which they will issue.

A recurrent image, that of the Two Eyes of the Sun and Moon Rising at the same time in the Eastern sky, prefigures the Rising of the brother-sister-lover-pairs, who come forth from the womb of night simultaneously, having already consummated their love whilst still in the womb. The Eldest son and daughter are destined to rule Egypt, founding the First Dynasty; likewise, the younger son and daughter are destined to marry and would always have held a place of honour in the land, if not for the younger son's subsequent treachery. Within these pairings, the archetypal patterns of day and night, light and dark, moist and dry are formulated. To Asar belongs the life-giving moist waters of the Nile; to Set, the parched desert; to Ast belongs the Dawn sky, to Neb-t het the pre-dawn and dusk. The balance is perfectly arranged and had it not been for the later jealous treachery of the younger brother, the Divine children would have dwelt in harmony, each with their rightful place. The Five Divine Children are Born on the final five consecutive days of the year and fall annually between August 24th-28th:

| August 24th | Birth of Asar, the Eldest Son, through marriage, ruler of Egypt. |
| August 25th: | Birth of Heru the Elder. |

August 26th	Birth of Set, the younger son.
August 27th	Birth of Ast, the Eldest Daughter, hereditary source of the Throne.
August 28th:	Birth of Neb-t het, the Younger Daughter and dark Twin.

That day and night, light and dark are both neutral should be clear from the fact that all are Children of the same womb, neither is 'good' or 'bad' at the time of birth. The Egyptian powers may be viewed as both objective and external beings existent within the Inner Planes, forces of nature and cosmos and also as highly subjective experiences and states of mind/being within the individual practitioner. It is because of this, that the Egyptian powers amy also be experienced in a distinctly Afrikan way - each Priestess or Priest having their 'own' Ast or Asar whom they serve and who manifests for them in a distinct pattern and who is formed out of the particular conjunction of pure and ancient archetypal energy manifesting through the physicality and psyche of each person, who themselves is an unique manifestation of hereditary intersecting with a particular time and place.

It is for this reason and the historical fact that the Egyptian rites have been continuously worked and re-worked since their encodement in the astral many thousands of years ago, that each practitioner seek to work with that purest form of the Gods and Goddesses and their rites. The pure archetypal image still contains encoded within it the ancient force and will unfold the old ways to those who seek persistently and with a pure heart. It is also for these reasons that no two practitioners could ever fully 'know' the Goddess the other serves and Ast utilizes the unique perspectives to accomplish her Work, which as will be realized by now, is multi-faceted and nigh all-encompassing.

The following praise-verse retells the Goddess quest at this modern time:

Through the Hours of the Night
 I have searched for you
Through the darkness guided by the Light
See! The temple blazes brightly
With many Lights to guide me
I search close and afar
For the Loved One ever in mind
You know your Name
I know you Name
Whispered into the depths of my being
I call it forth
Through the Hours of the Night
I search for you
See! The Temple blazes brightly to guide you home.

I have kept the vigil
Lit the candles
Sat by their Light
Through the Hours of the Night
Anubis guide me
Through corridors hidden
Warn me of danger
If I cannot see below.

Through the Hours of the Night
The Light was hidden in my body
Now Time comes to find me
To bring forth what is concealed
Lord Tehuti aid me with Wisdom and Words
Divine Power to create my True Destiny.

Through the Hours of the Night
I have searched for you
My love, my only one
Never doubt me
I am not thy betrayer
For your kisses are my nectar

Soothing away the scent of the Slayer
Lotus open upon the pond, receiving full Sun.

I have searched
I will find
Anubis to Guide me
Tehuti to advise
The Finding, the Creation, Life renewed by Love's touch.

Through the Hours of the Night
I have searched for you
Through the cold and the dark

I have longed for your touch
My holy star blazes from afar
Eternal emblem that the time comes
When reunited joy fills the Land.

Through the Hours of the Night
There is the Light of a Star
The Birth of a new Time arises
Where Love will lead, the Light will follow
It rains, a new day, the New Year arises.

(Inspired during Lychnapsia,1997).

2. Birthday of the Goddess Ast

"The beautiful day of the night of the Child in the cradle the
Great Festival of the entire world." [23]

It is with these words of praise and rejoicing from a Ptolemaic
fragment of unknown authorship, that the most important
Day within the Annual Ritual Cycle - that of the Birthday of
our Beloved Goddess Ast, is heralded.

This auspicious Celebration falls annually on our August 27th, the Fourth Intercalary Day and is a time for lavish feasting within the Shrine. In this festive and celebratory rite, we partake with the Goddess of Her Birthday Feast. In addition to the routine cleaning/sweeping of the Shrine, an extra effort should be made that a banquet truly fit for a Queen is presented with love and devotion, amidst an atmosphere of rejoicing befitting such an occasion. This is an ideal rite to invite friends and family, in addition to Priestesses, Priests and other devotees of Ast, or of other compatilble Godforms to attend.

Did you never realise that Ast, just like ourselves, has a Birthday? If not, then this is an excellent time to add this important date to your Ritual Calendar.

Some may ask, why bother celebrating the Goddess' Birthday? Isn't it a bit 'childish' and not 'high ceremonial'? Ask yourself, if you had close friends who guided and assisted you, perhaps teaching you and aiding you in other ways and then if you declared to them that they were of great importance to you - would you be likely to ignore their birthday? You probably wouldn't have that friend too long if you did! Amongst even casual acquaintances, the offering of a birthday goodwill is customary within modern society - why then, should the Goddess be treated in a manner less than we find acceptable?

How much more then, should we honour the arising, the birth, of the power with whom we seek favour!

Whilst celebrating the Birthdays of divinities is not featured as a practise within Western Traditions, it is a prominent feature of ancient Egyptian Temple rites, Ast being among many neter whose birthday is annually honoured (see also in this connection the lore surrounding the rise of Sep-t, also known as the Birthday of Het-heru).

Other cultures have maintained such rites up until the modern day, notably amongst the African Traditions which are flourishing within the Diaspora and also amongst Hindu practitioners and all honour to such Traditions and their devoted practitioners for maintaining the links with the ancient ways. It is through observation of such traditions, particularly those which have been practised in an unbroken lineage from Africa, that we, Western-born people, may perceive hints as to how the Egyptians - a North African people - may have approached and worshiped the divine realm, especially with rites such as Ast's Birthday, which have been 'lost' from view.

At some point, each of us needs to either keep working with the Egyptian powers in a Western way (i.e excluding rites such as this), or we need to make the conscious effort to disengage our preconceived notions and seek to approach the Egyptian powers in a manner more in keeping with their ancient identities.

Key Points For the Feast

1. Select foods and drinks from amongst Ast's favourite offerings (see *hetepu neter*).

2. All offerings should be presented in a dignified manner accompanied by ur *heka*.

3. A symbolic journey may be made, via a guided meditation, from Ast's Stellar Birthplace, Sep-t, to Her temple at Denderah (Her Birthplace upon Earth), then down the Nile, to our own astral Temple and from there to the physical Shrine we are within.

3. Rise of the Star Sep-t (Sirius)

Having kept the vigil of the final twelve days of the ancient Egyptian Calendar - August 12th-24th the Sun beginning within the zodiac constellation of Leo; then changing into Virgo around the 23rd-24th August each year; both the Intercalary Days and the subsequent Rise of Sep-t also occur whilst the Sun is in Virgo. August 29th on our calendar corresponds to the Egyptian New Years' Day; within the fixed Alexandrian Calendar this day was also known as Thoth 1, the months being named after the deities.

The annual Rise of Sep-t is a celestial occurrence of paramount importance in both the sacred and secular workings of Egypt: its rise heralded not only a New Year, but also the timing of each successive Pharoah ascending to his throne; this day also marked the Birthday of Het-heru (Hathor). In a very literal manner, Hathor's primary Temple at Denderah was the location of the birthplace of the New Year and the sanctioning of Pharoah's ascent to power. In an earlier chapter it was highlighted that this Temple at Denderah had been aligned to the Rise of Sep-t at the time of its construction and it is within this Temple, that the famous 'Denderah Zodiac' was originally erected. This circular Zodiac commemorates a pivotal celestial occurrence and also acts as a timekeeper portraying the cycle which the Sun which arises on this New Year's Day, must pass through before being annually reborn. That this Temple is aligned to both Rise of the Sun and Rise of the Star Sep-t, is also confirmed by this being Het- heru's domain and She is both the House of the Rising Sun, Horus and in another aspect is portrayed as a reclining Cow crowned with the Star Sep-t.

That the 'official' Rise of Sep-t, New Year and the enthronement of the Pharoah are all timed together on this day is both significant and necessary; for the sister-lover-mother Ast must be born first to enable the Sun/son Child to come forth and also practically as She is the Throne which he must ascend. The Denderah Zodiac portrays in symbolic language the actual means of this ascension, this Rising in the Eastern quadrant portrays the Solar Hawk and the Stellar Cow Rise simultaneously.

The impact of the single-point of ancestral stellar light-energy converging with the incarnate Sun-god at this time and the power this would encode into each successive year, cycle, Pharoah can only be implied in the fruits of the Dynastic times: the Wisdom teachings which remain to today a source of genuine Initiatory power and insight; the monuments beyond the scope of even modern construction; the art and artifacts all lend a weighty testimony that there was an enormous spiritual and occult power directing the civilisation.

It is fitting too, that the Rise of Sep-t also announced the onset of the annual rainy season, the inundation which flooded the Nile annually fecundating the land. This celestial outpouring is suggestive of the spiritual fecundation which also occurred on this day. Without exaggeration, the Rise of Sep-t brought immense ancestral forces to incarnation; the Divine ancestors being reborn in their earthly counterparts. This star is the light of both temporal and spiritual power, elemental blessing, abundance; its' Rise being the cause for rejoicing annually.

That the Enthronement of each Pharoah took place on this day gives insight into the meaning of the Rising of this star: to 'Rise' equates with both ascending to power and the physical act of enthronement - a literal ascending of the Throne. As has been revealed, this Throne is the Goddess Ast and the 'Rising' of New Year's Day is also an allusion to the brother-sister marriage - the Rite by which the brother was empowered as the new Pharoah being a hierogamos.

It must never be forgotten that the actual power of the Egyptian Throne was the Goddess Ast in Dynastic periods and that without the brother-sister marriage, no male could rule. The great love for Her brother Asar, evidenced throughout the long nights of the preceding Lychnapsia is rewarded with the Finding of the God - with His Birth on August 24th, which parallels the rising of the Sun after the twelve hours of the night.

The subsequent bestowal of the Throne upon Her brother and later, after His murder, upon their son as the re-incarnation of His father, is also an act of love; for Ast could have continued to rule the Two Lands as she had previously done successfully when Asar travelled abroad. This fact did not go unnoticed by later royal women, who utilizing this archetypal pattern decided to rule in their own right as Pharaoh, rather than having the brother-son-lover 'sit in their lap'. An example of such a female Horus is Hat-shepsut; an Eighteenth Dynasty ruler also known by the Throne-name of Maat-ka-Ra II [24]. The reason for highlighting this historically significant fact is to emphasise the full import of the power of Ast's stellar birthplace,Sep-t (or Sirius); for this star is truly the birthplace and source of the power of the Egyptian Mysteries and these, powers are fully available, in fact are incarnated or brought to Earth through the female adept within whom the powers of the Goddess Ast are focused.

Within Hatshepsut's Throne name this mystery is revealed, for the Goddess Maat, the sister and daughter is the ka, or spiritual double and genius of the father, Ra, incarnating His powers: this is an ancient mystery containing a Truth (Maat) that must be spoken. It is very necessary at this end of Millennia to rectify the imbalance that has crept in and been maintained throughout the centuries in the perception of the role of both the goddess and of women within both ancient Egypt and within hierarchies which themselves take the form of 'spiritual Egypts'. Nowhere is the Goddess' full importance and power highlighted greater than within the complex of symbolism surrounding each New Year.

Aligned to this auspicious and powerful day is the Jackal Lord Anpu. Earlier the circumstances surrounding Anpu's conception, birth and subsequent adoption by Ast have been described (see Chapter Rite of Descent). In His role as a Necropolis Guardian and Guide within the ancestral regions, Anpu becomes one of the most powerful and beneficent God-forms, who encompasses within Himself the ability to not only Guard and Guide, but to Show the Way and to Open the Doors a subtle and important difference in roles: it is for these reasons that Anpu is often addressed as the 'Opener of the Ways' in ritual. The 'Door' that He Opens is a concealed one and becomes apparent only at the liminal times of dusk and dawn; this is the Door of the Horizon, the line between Day and Night, Above and Below. Anpu's close connection with the star Sep-t is underlined by reference to the time of Sep-t's rising in July (remember the Egyptian Calendar has three 'risings') and preceding the Inundation, being called the Dog-days.

The placement upon the Tree of Life for Sirius is at Da'ath: Knowledge in its purest sense of being the Knowledge of both Above and Below, of the realms of Life and of Death. Da'ath as a stellar gateway into the Tuat, is experienced directly by the experience of visionary dreams and night-journeys. An experience of the interconnection of these matters may be obtained through the Pathworking associated with the High Priestess card, Atu II in tarot; another title for which is the Priestess of the Silver Star - the star referred to being Sep-t. Within this card the Goddess Ast is portrayed upon the Throne of Her name and correctly positioned, as the sephira Da'ath is upon the Tree, with reference to and between the sephira of Binah and Chokmah, represented as two pillars one black (Binah) and the other white (Chokmah). Naturally there are also many other meanings behind these powerful symbols. What is of interest to the quest for the Knowledge of Sep-t is that the Goddess-Priestess is enthroned and veiled; the enthronement itself being a glyph for the Rising of the

Star and the veil itself being emblematic of the stellar luminescence which accompanies the enthronement-rise of Sirius and which always conceals the bright-darkness of Her True face - which is imageless.

If you carefully look at the placement of the Gimel pathway, the pathway which flows directly from the Atziluthic realm of the first sephiroth Kether, through and across Da'ath and the line of the abyss, down to manifestation within the realm of Tiphareth, the Solar sphere; you will also become aware that the Goddess-Priestess' robe becomes fluid, creating a river; this too is symbolic and in one way may be seen as representative of the annual rains of the Inundation which accompanies the rise of Sep-t. On the personal level, this is representative of that great outpouring of Knowledge which accompanies the successful accomplishment of the works associated with Tiphareth and which in every way parallel Ast's seeking and finding of Her Beloved. The position upon the Tree reaffirms the role which Sep-t plays in linking the powers of the Divine, archetypal realms with those of humanity, of linking the Macrocosm with the

Microcosm; of aspirant with their God; of self with beloved and beyond this, of linking us with the timeless and invisible realms beyond. In this connection it is worth noting that Lord Anpu's Temple was anciently a place where devotees went for dream-Incubations after an act of ritualised sex with a Priest, who in full Jackal headdress, incarnated the God. This practise continued down to Roman times and was discontinued after a Roman political figure payed one of the Priests to let him take the role of the God so that he could sleep with the wife of a rival political figure whom he lusted after. When this deception and misuse of religious rite was uncovered, the Temple and its priesthood were dealt with harshly.

The interconnection of the motif of death, in the form of the Necropolis Guardian and Tuat Guide and sex is one made explicitly within many cultures; sex being the physical vehicle whereby new life may return from the ancestral regions: the God must die to enable rejuvenation and renewal of His form. It is literally true that the source of all life is sexual and this aspect is referenced within the symbolism and lore surrounding the Rise of Sep-t.

For ceremonial purposes, Lord Anpu may be potently honoured as a God-form encompassing both protection, Tuat Journeys, dream oracles and sexual mysteries.His form is as amorphous as His mother's and so Lord Anpu becomes a patron and tutelary god-form who Guides and Guards practitioners of all sexualities; the gender-fluidity and otherworldly sexual nature of many of the primary Egyptian god-forms being both abundantly testified to and acknowledged in an earlier Chapter.

Here follows a list of the primary hieroglyphic forms of the Goddess, which reveal both her amorphous nature and the close relationship with Anpu and the realms just discussed. Accompanying each form is an allocation to a particular realm within the Egyptian world-view and to a kabbalistic sphere of working. It is hoped that this cross-referencing will enable practitioners more familiar with one system or the other, to get a grasp of the breadth and depth of Ast's domain and also the key role which the Rise of Sep-t and the star itself play within unlocking Her deeper mysteries.

Second Key
The Hieroglyphic Forms of Ast as Utilized in the Ancient Egyptian Temples

Ast Ament-t   (T)(TuatV-Isis in the Kingdom of
                     Seker)Da'ath

Ast Anpu	(T)(Seat of Anpu / an alternate Royal Throne)Da'ath
Ast ur-t mut neter	(E)(Isis the Great, Mother of the God) Binah
Ast em neb-t ankh	(E)(Isis Lady of Life/9th Hour of the day)
Ast em sem-t	(E)
Ast em Ta-tcheser	(E)(Isis in the Holy Land)
Ast Mehit	(T)(TuatVI, a northern form)
Ast netrit-em renus-nebu	(E)(Isis in all names)Hod
Ast netchit	(T)(TuatII, Isis the Avenger with knife-shaped phallus) Da'ath
Ast Septit	(S)(Isis Sothis)Da'ath
Ast ta-uh	(A)(Scorpion Isis)Geburah
Ast-uraeus	(A)(In the Solarboat, a Tuat aspect) Chokmah,Da'ath
Ast-Rait-set	(A)(A lioness-headed form)Tiphareth
Ast-Heru	(E)(Seat of Horus/the Royal Throne) Binah, Tiphareth
Ur-urti	(E)(A title of Isis and Nepthys)
Neb-t aakhu	(T)(TuatXI, a Serpent dawn Goddess) Da'ath
Urit-hekau	(E)(A name of the Crown of the South or of its Goddess) Hod
ur-heka	(All)(The Words of Power)
Neter mut	(E/A)(Divine Mother, a Vulture-form) Binah
Ast meskhen-t en Ast	(E)(Isis' Birthplace, Denderah)
Ast au ab	(E)(Seat of the Heart, Denderah) Tiphareth
Ast aab-s Het-Her	(E)(Seat of the Heart of Het-Heru) Tiphareth
Ast sekhem ankh r en nete	(All)(Isis of Vital Force and Divine Life) Middle Pillar
Ast uab	(E) ("Holy Place"- Philae)Malkuth

Ast enth hem-t nesu* (E) (Seat of the Queen /Denderah) Binah
*nesu is the Royal sign related to Upper Egypt.

Key to Aspects

(A) = Anthropomorphic, animal
(E) = Earth, Land of Egypt
(S) = Sky, stellar
(T) = Tuat, the ancestral regions

An experiential allocation to a sephiroth upon the Otz Chiim(Tree of Life) follows the translation of each name to enable placement of Ast's forces and forms kabbalistically. [25]

4. Veiling of the Goddess

The season of Akhe, the Inundation commences auspiciously with the Rise of Sep-t and the subsequent Enthronement of Pharoah; this takes place at the beginning of September. However the renewal of power, felt on a large and public scale accompanying these Celebrations, ultimately demand that the Old God die again in order to perpetuate the Cycle the following year. It is for this reason, that the final Month of the Inundation, December, sees the Goddess again Mourning the loss of her Beloved, who was slain in the preceding Month.

On one level, this is synonymous and symbolic of the Annual Harvest Rites which are to follow during Winter. On another level, the timing of the Death and Re-birth of the God in the renewed form of the Child -Heru, the Pharoah, means that Annually, He is nine months within the ancestral regions, ruling as King of Amen-t. The direct parallel with the facts of nature and pregnancy requiring nine months, speaks of Asar's sojourn in the Lands to the West as being a time when He experiences deep renewal within the womb of the inner Earth.

It is at Solstice time, that the annual Veiling of the Goddess is performed. The custom of annually bringing the God/Goddess forth from within their Shrine in a public display, reaffirmed to the Egyptian people that the neters remained amongst them.

Unlike other joyous Rites involving Ast in Her Solar-Cow Transformation, such as the Annual drunken rituals of Hetheru; when Ast is brought forth from the Shrine at this time, it is a solemn public event and marks the commencement of a symbolic period of Mourning for the Goddess as She searches for Her lost love.

The recumbent statue of the Goddess in her Cow-form is veiled in Black and carried solemnly Seven times around the temple on each of Seven successive days. This is observed in silence by the people, who understand that the Goddess is like them, in that She, too is a woman who has experienced love and endured loss. This aspect of the Goddess gives great hope to her followers, who rightly believe that She will grant favour to those who call upon Her in need.

However, the Veiling of the Goddess, the external sign of Mourning, is accompanied, within Her Temple by darkness - no lights are lit during these days. Ast's Mourning, in one form, leads to the annual flooding of the Nile as She seeks to find Asar. However, the placement and and dating of this festival at the time of Winter Solstice, echoes similar observances in other ancient cultures; where the re-birth of the God is annually preceded by days of darkness and silence. Whilst known widely as this aspect, the 'Mourning Isis' is in reality only one aspect out of many which She annually embodies. Whilst She may appear as a Goddess of Sorrows at this time, She is not an eternally grieving Goddess-form to work with. In this form, it may be beneficent for women to take comfort from the Goddess' experiences and Her deep understanding of emotional sorrows, places Her as a Goddess who may be turned to in times of need. Especially important at this time is the realization that this is a phase of Her Annual Ritual Cycle which should not be unnecessarily prolonged, as this would suppress the manifestation of her other, creative aspects.

Allow Seven days to Perform the Veiling, one day for each of the Seven forms of the Cow-Goddess, who presides over re-birth and birthing in general, but also symbolic of one-quarter of a Lunar Cycle, when the God's Light is hidden from view at the Waning phase. During this time, any statue of the Goddess upon the Altar should be fully covered with a Black Cloth and no lights or incense lit within the Shrine.

This is a time of quiet and solemnity and provides an ideal opportunity to engage in works of self-healing; particularly from past emotional distresses. In this way this time can be viewed as a period of cleansing.

Viewed individually each of these Festivals of the Annual Calendar provide a self-contained observance, complete with Traditional lore and accompanying practises.

Viewed as a whole Cycle, which these observances are all interconnected parts, what emerges is a reaffirmation of the principles of both Ascent and Descent and the alternate seasonal blending of Light and Dark aspects, which enable the total of life to be renewed. In celebrating the full Annual Cycle, we systematically and ceremonially traverse the Two Lands, cleansing, illuminating, celebrating, mourning and raising power from both the heights of heaven and the depths of the Tuat. it is this potent and cyclic intermingling of the dual powers of Life and death which effect a renewal of all conscious life: nature, animal, human and divine - all partake in the renewal of the Shrine.

The potential cumulative benefits of enacting this cycle over many years and in Egyptian times, many generations, for both the individual and society should be clearly hinted at. For here we have before us an ancient and authentic, divine Cycle of renewal; luminous in its shining and yet still concealing hidden treasures for each succeeding generation to personally unlock within the shadows of that light. So like Ast, let each one be able to say through the Darkness and the Light 'I have sought you and have found you in the hidden recesses of my heart'.

5. The Pleophesia

Three months after the time of Mourning, March 5th sees the Winter Harvest Festival arrive. Of all the Annual Festivals, this is perhaps the most widely known - the annual offering of a barge which was set forth to Sea laden with choice *hetepu neter*, was devoted and released to Ast to invoke Her blessing upon the commencement of the annual sailing season. It is quite likely, that a distant remembrance of this time, remains today within the secular custom of 'blessing all new boats with spirit (i.e alcohol)', such boats often being called a woman's name.

Though later in origin than the Lighting of the Lamps, this festival holds significance as a time when there was great public rejoicing. Of the Annual Festivals held in Ast's honour, those of Summer and the East ironically have a much more private, or hidden aspect, being performed indoors within the Temple. By comparison, the Winter Rites see a large, festive crowd gathering in joyous processional to attend upon their Queen. The sheer size and scale of such Festivals and the resources which are required to stage them effectively, could also be one of the reasons behind the ancient Temples having a balance between the large and small rites annually.

The symbolism of the Barge, or Boat, which is annually set sail, works on both the obvious (public) level as a Rite of Sympathetic magick ensuring a fecund sailing/fishing season and yet there are deeper allusions here in the symbolism of the Boat as explored further in Chapter 9, Rite of Ascent. Ast's connection with the Ocean, through sailors utilising her Star to navigate provides an additional metaphor underpinning the use of the Boat as the means to Journey into Stellar realms.

The Boat has other layers of symbolism and significance and through the focus upon the Ocean, the Great Sea, at this time Ast connection to Binah is reaffirmed; with the symbolism of fishing and similar allusions to fecundity suggestive of Ast in the Bright, Fertile Binah form. It must be called to mind here, that the primordial sea, the Waters of Chaos are the origin of life and containing all possibilities, provides a symbol of immense creative potential to draw from Ast's Boat on another level can be interpreted as a primal Womb.

Over time, the Goddess' connection in the popular imagination with this large Festival, enabled the Greek Priests to sidetrack attention away from the more ancient Tuat and Stellar connections; until Isis was thought of as a Lunar Goddess, due to the Moon's connection with the Ocean tides, rather than the original and inner attribution of Her as an Earth-Sky-Tuat divinity, who manifested Her Sky and Tuat force within the form of a Stellar Queen with regard to the Sea. This occurred despite the remarkable fact that Truth of Her character was known to them and contemporary Greek Historians, such as Plutarch, publically remarked upon Osiris (Asar) being a Lunar God.

Unfortunately, Ast spanned too many realms and presented an immense image of female power and this did not fit in with the amalgamation of the Egyptian Religion by the Greek at the outset and continuing during the Ptolemaic Dynasties. It is a prayer of the ancient ones, that all who enter the Temple will become a speaker of Truth, one whose Words are True; in revealing that Isis had a more ancient and often vastly different form than what has been popularly remembered, a Truth is being spoken today, which stands up to scrutiny and investigation from both a magickal and an Egyptological - historical perspective. Perhaps the information regarding Ast's more ancient characteristics and manifestations out-lined within this book, will in some small way contribute to re-instating Ast's within Her ancient forms today, so many centuries since they had been deliberately hidden (by the Greek Priests) to a wider view. Those who work with Her as a Lunar Goddess, rather than denying all of the Goddess' char-acteristics, will perhaps be interested in exploring Her in these other forms in the light of the information presented. Highly suited to a public and group endeavour, this is a Festival for both young and old, those unfamiliar with Egyptian Rites and those who already practise within the Tradition. It is an accessible an d beneficial Rite to enact on a large scale, so that the benefits of this time may encompass a broader base of society.

Key Elements of the Festival

* The construction of a large and ornate ceremonial Barge

* Preparation of a large feast and offerings which are heaped upon the Barge

* A large and joyous procession carrying the Barge to the Ocean

* Setting the Barge afloat accompanied with prayers and requests for Ast's blessing

* The loud proclamation of the word 'Pleophesia !' which officially begins the Harvest /Sailing Season.

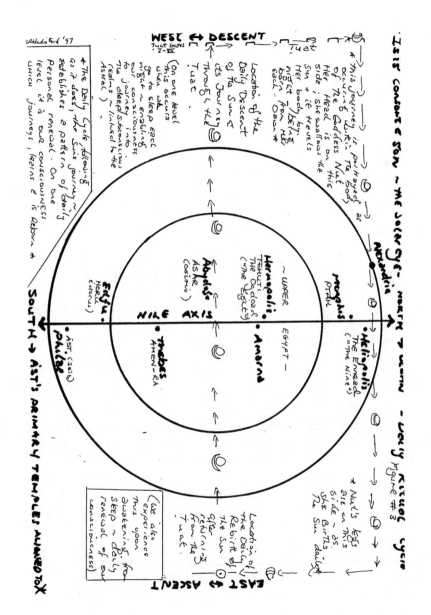

8.

The Incubation Sleep

Sleep daughter, sleep - do not be afraid
for in the dark, the deep
all things are born, all things re-made' - Ast.

In the service of Ast, times arise when it is not the Priestess, Priest, or devotee who expends their energy within the Shrine - but it is Isis Herself who performs the Work. It is in times of deep need that the full love and care of the Goddess for those within Her House manifests itself and may be experienced in the forms of healing and the receiving of guidance in the form of dream oracles. the use of sleep as a healing and divinatory rite has many ancient precedents.

When in the dream state, the subconscious mind is free to both roam the Inner Planes of the astral realm and also be open to receiving inspiration and direction from those realms. Because of the connection between the lower astral realms and the emotional level of the individual, imbalances within the emotional life of the practitioner can have adverse effects upon the astral realms; in the same manner that creating disturbances in the astral will adversely effect the practitioner and may manifest in a variety of ways including poor health. For anything to manifest in the outer world and in the life of the practitioner it must first have worked its way out from within the mind to the emotional level of the practitioner and from there onto the astral, where its' astral form finds a later release within physical manifestation within the world of matter, the plane of existences.

Understanding the interrelationship between the conscious mind, the thoughts it seeds into the subconscious and then the work the subconscious fulfils in transmitting these thoughts in the form of an emotional charge out onto the astral where they take a take a form that may then be mirrored into the everyday world, is essential to use of sleep as a ritual technique.

Within the safety, both physical and astral, of the Temple; the practitioner may experience the guidance of the Goddess in the form of seeking dream oracles through the ancient rite of the Incubation Sleep, either as a solo rite or group rite, or through being guided into such a sleep by a Priestess (Please note this is not a form of hypnosis, with the correlating loss of self-direction and will that hypnosis implies.) The one seeking the healing vision or the divinatory dream oracle would consult closely with the mediating Priest/ess as to the focus of the sleep and corresponding dream induction would be created to suit this; once the candidate is asleep, the Priest/ess would withdraw, or sit in vigil depending on the goal of the sleep. For instance, in the cases of healing sleep, it may be appropriate to stay and monitor the candidate, keep incense burning and otherwise be alert for any signs. As with other areas of magickal work, the ritual area should be thoroughly cleaned, cleansed and consecrated, with only items indicative of the goal left in the room, which should otherwise be free of clutter and distraction.

In times of great distress, loss, bereavement or mental anguish, the experience of spending a night (or, nights) within the Temple in an Incubation Sleep can be a means of assisting in stabilising one's life. In these cases, it is recommended that an experienced Priestess place the person within the Shrine and watch over them as they rest. This can be accompanied by gentle invocations to Ast on behalf of the distressed one, seeking their healing. This experience of loving support within a sacred environment cannot be described fully in words and has many potential positive effects.

An experienced practitioner may safely embark upon an Incubation Sleep solo, utilising their connection to the Shrine (which is always an outer manifestation of themselves) to guide them. The use of candles to illumine the darkness is recommended for those times when healing is sought; at other times it is recommended that the Shrine be left dark, that it may better serve as an incubatory womb. It is also suggested that the bedding fully envelopes the sleeper, that they are snugly wrapped with only their head exposed. If mediating this rite for someone else,it is easy to wrap them closely. For a solo Incubation, bedding such as a sleeping-bag provides an ideal environment. This style of bedding is symbolically akin to mummification and the preparation for the descent of the mind into the ancestral realms of Amen-t that mummification also signifies.

This realm of Amen-t, presided over by Ast's beloved Asar (Osiris), is also the Tuat region over which She shares dominion. The daily journey of the Sun from its rising in the East and movement across the heavens before descending into the Western regions of the Tuat at dusk, is also symbolic of the journey the consciousness of each individual makes daily: we rise when we awake from sleep, we journey through our daily lives and we descend into the night-time realm of the subconscious, land of the ancestors, of dreaming, of sleep and there another journey takes place before we awake refreshed.

In this connection, the Tuat becomes recognizable as the deep recesses of our own minds, inner space, our subconscious. As such, the reading of texts such as the Book of Going Forth By Day (i.e. the "Book of the Dead") and the detailed descriptions of both the horrors and the pleasures of the Egyptian after-life, begin to take on different and personal meanings. For whilst we acknowledge that the Tuat exists as a realm in its own right, that may be journeyed to and where the ancient Egyptian powers dwell, it is important to also understand that a form of the Tuat also resides within the deep mind of each practitioner and that it can be accessed through the gateway of the dream-state. In this regard, it is highly suitable that a consecrated image or statue of Lord Anpu (Anubis) be located somewhere within the bed-chamber, or in the Shrine during an Incubation Sleep; for as has be discussed earlier, Anpu is the Guardian of the Gateway, located at the Horizon - where the Sun both rises and sets. In other words, He is the most suitable god-form to invoke for Guidance as we seek to descend into the mysteries of the night, for he is positioned at exactly the place where our conscious and subconscious minds meet.

Preparation for an Incubation Sleep may be either complex or simple depending upon the requirements of the time. Bathing in a ritual bath,which contains rock salt (added whilst the water is flowing, with a Banishing gesture) and Anise (added whilst the water is flowing with an Invocation suited to the occasion) prior to sleep serves two purposes: it cleanses the body physically and spiritually and it also relaxes the body and mind making it more receptive to sleep. Have the bedding prepared within the Shrine prior to the bath, so that you may go straight from the bath to the Incubation bed. The Incubation may be performed as required,or planned for a particular day of the week to align it to a planet or aspect of Ast relevant the goal of the Incubation (see tables in other chapters).

Incense should then be chosen (or not) to amplify the atmosphere. In times of distress a purificatory scent is recommended, particularly Myrrh. At other times, Khyphi will create a dignified atmosphere; whilst Cyprus and Violet create a gentler atmosphere, very conducive to sleep. Herbs used widely within the Western Mysteries for dreamwork, such as mugwort, may also be utilised. Whilst it may be more potent to use herbs/resins pleasing and recognizable to Ast Traditionally, as it is She whom we seek within the darkness for healing and to bestow the dream oracle; the multiple aspects which She presents in and the accompanying herb/resin correspondences throughout time would undoubtedly reveal that at one time or another She has been called with most plants/incenses known. It is therefore suggested that the practitioner descend into the Dream Incubation accompanied by a scent they love best.

9.

Ríte of Ascent

The extent to which the affairs of Egypt were overseen and regulated by the divine realms becomes apparent when the many areas referred to and named as gods and goddesses is seen. From the measurement of the royal cubit - where each of its twenty-eight finger-breadths is a god or goddess; to the hours of both day and night and the months of the year, each of these is named and revered as being under the guardianship of a divine being; whose source of power and origin were ultimately seen to be derived from their stellar namesake. For the ancient Egyptians, the stars were the overlighting and guiding principle of those times; while the Outer mysteries publically viewed were a cult of the Sun, the Inner Temple tradition is essentially stellar - to the priestly class the stars themselves being viewed as the manifest Light of the gods and goddesses. In this way, very literally is Egypt a place of the gods - for there is no aspect of life that does not fall under their domain.

It is for this reason that an examination of the Zodiac sculpture which was upon the roof of Ast's sacred temple at Denderah provides both a key and a guide into those realms.The Denderah Zodiac "is said to represent midnight of the Summer Solstice, 700 B.C., when Sirius rose at dawn with the sun".[1] This aspect is featured on the right side of the Zodiac, in the middle, in the form of a seated cow with a star and horn headdress (i.e Sirius) beside a hawk wearing the

Double Crown atop a sceptre (i.e. the Sun). In addition to this and the clear depiction of the twelve constellations of the zodiac known both anciently and to us, several other important features are notable:

1. That it is a map of the land Of Upper Egypt, beginning with the Khemenu (the Ogdoad, the primeval Eight), seen to the left of the Zodiac encircled. When a map of Egypt is transposed onto this Zodiac, it becomes apparent that this aligns with the area where Upper Egypt begins and which was called Hermopolis by the Greeks; being the place of the sacred word the utterance of which begins Creation and is under the auspices of Lord Tehuti (Gk.Thoth). Lower Egypt is not depicted on the Zodiac. This fact is not unusual when you consider that it is a celestial map from the point of view of the Temple revered as the Birthplace of the Mother Goddess of the Upper Land.

2. That each Temple which flanks either the East or West bank of the Nile is also depicted in its correct position, utilising an animal transformation appropriate to the tutelary god/goddess to whom the temple is dedicated. (see Diagrams of the Land of Egypt and the Zodiac).

3. This suggests that either (a) the Zodiac was drawn after the Dynasties had been around a long time, having built the temples; whilst the date ascribed to the Zodiac supports this - in this case whilst the Zodiac would relate the the physical land of Egypt, it would not relate to the areas of the sky astronomically, unless (b) the sky/stars had been observed at length over many generations to enable an exact position upon the earth to be marked out prior to construction of the temples. In this way, each Temple would be located in alignment with the stellar home of its tutelary divinity; the Temple

itself being a fixed earthly home for the stellar powers, which were symbolized in the religion as gods and goddesses in animal forms. That many Temples did in fact receive a great irradiation from the rising light of a particular star, at least once a year, offers a practical basis in support of this theory. The connection between the emergence of the Dynasties and the construction of these fixed monuments - some built as shrines to particular aspects of the divine, others built to receive the body of the Pharoah and the Queen, these being the incarnated gods and goddesses - and the shift away from the pre-Dynastic nomadic existence, is also suggestive of the careful and conscious creation of permanent earth-based receptors/transmitters of the celestial power.

4. It becomes apparent when looking closely at both the Daily and the Annual Ritual Cycles enacted in the Temples sacred to Ast at both Philae and Denderah, that they enable the entire Zodiac - and thus also the land of Egypt - to be symbolically and ceremonially circumambulated at least once each year; enabling the great work of renewing the life of the Temple (the divine realm, the lands of Egypt, the people). (see "Daily" and "Annual Ritual Cycle" diagrams).

The interrelationship between the daily and the yearly rites reflects a pattern of wholeness and attunement to sources of great power and equilibrium.

Just as Ast is both Goddess and Queen of three realms - Earth, Sky and Tuat; so Her ritual calendar honours these realms season by season. The ancient Egyptian calendar consisted of three seasons of four months, each thirty days long (making 360 days) followed by the five Intercalary days when the five children of Nut and Geb were born (365 days in total). The annual cycle commenced with the season of the

Inundation or Akhe; the Inundation itself being heralded by the Rising of the star Sep-t * (Sirius). This powerful and auspicious New Year's Day was known as wpt-rnpt and was also the day when each successive Pharoah was enthroned. The second season was Winter orProye and the third season, preceding the wpt-rnpt, was Summer orShomu. Each of these seasons can be aligned to one of the three realms: Akhe to the Tuat; Proye to Earth (and Sea): Shomu to the Sky. As with other aspects of the Egyptian religion, these alignments follow a natural and logical pattern, the annual calendar being a microcosmic mirror of the natural and celestial worlds.

The cycle of Descent and return (Inundation-early Winter) is naturally followed with the large public festivals of rejoicing and offerings; these are the times of the ancestors (Tuat) returning bring back the fecundity of the land (Earth) as the Nile floods. As the year turns, these public ceremonies give way to smaller, private Temple Rites of Ascent focused upon stellar Light (Sky realm). The important Lighting of the Lamps ceremony previously worked with symbolized the annual renewal of the Unification of the Two Lands, being celebrated in the Temples of the Goddess of the North, Neith (Cobra-Uadjit/ Uraeus) and the Goddess of the South, Ast (Vulture-Nekhbet) simultaneously. The Lighting of these Lamps also foreshadowed the Rising of the Celestial 'Lamp', Sirius (compare one of the hieroglyphs used to refer to star =a 'sky-lamp'). At this time of Summer, the emphasis on the elements of air (Sky) and fire (flame, lamps, stellar lore, star-rising) provides an elemental completion to the cycle which saw the Winter rites focused upon the elements of earth (harvest) and water (the Ship offerings). In this way, the two seasons which we are used to, Summer and Winter, enable the elements to be worked with in a natural sequence;Summer Rites of Ascent, of air and fire precede Creation (Birth of the Five gods and goddesses; re-birth of the god in the form of the Pharoah; the New Year); whilst Winter Rites of earth and water, show forth the fruits of the renewal of Creation. Winter is neither a time of ascent or descent, but marks the place between; this is the time of the Land of Egypt itself. This tripartite division of both divine realms and seasonal times enables each practitioner to attune to and strengthen their connection with the elements within the framework of the larger ritual cycle.

The interconnectedness of human and divine realms is also emphasised when you realise that this annual cycle of ceremonies is based upon the same pattern as the Land of Egypt itself:

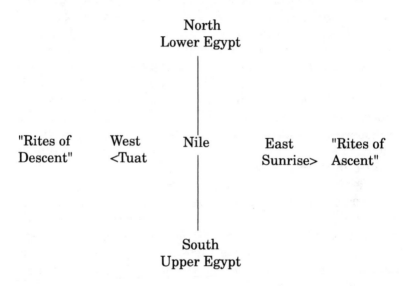

North
Lower Egypt

"Rites of   West   Nile   East   "Rites of
Descent"   <Tuat   Sunrise>   Ascent"

South
Upper Egypt

The first season, the Inundation, parallels the physical Nile and the ceremonies of this season link to the West, the Royal Necropolis and further West, beyond the mountains, the Immeasurable Region of the Egyptian Otherworld the Tuat. Contrasting with this are the Rites of Ascent and Summer, which parallel the East, the Abode of Sunrise - place of the daily re-birth of the Light. In between these seasons and rites of Below and Above are the Winter Rites which echo the daily activities along the banks of the Nile itself, such as farming and further North still, the fishing and sailing which brought trade from distant lands.

It is important to establish the connections between the ritual cycles, seasons and realms and to understand that the annual cycle of rituals echoes the daily cycle, on another level traversing a metaphysical landscape, which like the ritual calendar itself, is firmly based upon the physical geography of Egypt. The Daily Rites directly link self and sun and may be undertaken for personal renewal of consciousness.Similarly the Annual Rites which connect the Land and Stellar/ Ancestral realms may be undertaken as a means to link the self with the macrocosm. Anciently the annual rites were enacted for the benefit of the whole society, they are of a more transpersonal nature. Each cycle reinforces and renews the other. That the physical terrain of the Two Lands and the daily and yearly movements of the Sun, Moon and Stars provided the cosmography and geography of Tuat also cannot be overemphasised - one realm mirrors the other.In this connection, the Land of Egypt itself is the earthly counterpart of the stellar regions as has been discussed. Through this powerful interplay between the celestial, terrestrial and ancestral, a union of forces between these three realms is achieved and maximised.

It is this geography - a living river coursing through its centre and protected by a mountainous region to both the East and the West - that provides one of the reasons why the culture flourished powerfully for so long. With constant revitalisation at its centre the valley which Egypt was nestled amidst both conducted energy and was able to transmit that energy from higher realms.

Through a close and deep meditation upon both the daily and annual ritual cycles, when viewed as a three-dimensional model, with the Denderah Zodiac Above and a map of the Land of Egypt Below, yields meaningful insights. Each realm is seen to be a mirror-image of the other - but on another level - enabling work with each level both successively and consecutively. The suggested three-dimensional model may be achieved by overlaying the diagrams provided in the following manner:

Aethyr	Denderah Zodiac	= Creative Source
Air	Annual Rites Renewal & Stellar Illumination	= Archetypal Realm Higher Guides Superconscious
Water &Fire	Daily Rites	= Conscious and Subconscious
	Journey of the Sun & Moon	Astral
Earth	Map of Egypt	= Physical Plane

If these four layers are envisioned as circles decreasing in size from the largest, the Zodiac, to the smallest, the map of Egypt; it also becomes apparent that the energy of the Stellar regions - through the annual and the daily rites - becomes focused upon and within the Earth plane (i.e. Egypt). This has practical applications for modern practitioners, in that a similar effect (on a microcosmic scale) can be achieved by the conscious construction of the individual Temple, in alignment with these principles.

As the daily rites follow the actual course of the Sun and Moon over the Land of Egypt, sinking into the Western mountains and being daily reborn beyond the Eastern Mountains. Similarly, the annual rites lead the practitioner through the terrain of Egypt - enabling connection and work with the powers which it embodies, revealing aspects of individual consciousness which coincide. When these 'maps' are aligned so that the Eastern regions of each are aligned with each other, other interesting features are revealed. For example, if you trace the daily and nightly journeys of the sun over the map of Egypt, a sacred geometry emerges in a rectangular form (see 'Daily Ritual Cycle' diagram). It is this geometry which provided one of the bases of the floorplan of the Temple (refer chapter. 3. the Temple Service).

In this connection, the Land of Egypt itself is the earthly counterpart and 'temple' of the stellar regions above. It is upon this celestial vision that the allocation and positioning of Temple sites flanking each bank of the Nile was decided; enabling a symmetry with the stellar homes of the various goddesses and gods who dwelt within. As a useful exercise, set out to be able to identify these for yourself utilising the Denderah Zodiac and a knowledge of which animal transformation each divine force manifested in anthropo-morphically - the reality of this 'Above and Below' symmetry becomes rapidly apparent. The Nile itself could be said to find its celestial home in the once circumpolar stars of the constellation Draco; through the representation of the Nile's largest inhabitant the Hippopotomus. In the Zodiac the Hippopotomus is the central animal form and signifies Taur-t Ast. Together, this constellation and the nearby Ursa Major and Ursa Minor (the Greater and Lesser Bears) form the region of stars closest to the Northern Pole of the Heavens and the Pole-Star - Stella Polaris. Het-heru's (Hathor's) Temple at Denderah was aligned to these central stars and was representative of the Goddess in Her most secret and illuminating form. As has been mentioned, Denderah was also the location of the Annual hierogamos rites; represented outwardly through the union of the Hawk from Heru's temple at Edfu, with the Goddess' Hawk which lived in the Denderah Temple. Denderah was also revered as the Birthplace of Ast upon Earth. The depiction of both the Sun and Sirius 'rising' at the same time and the astrological occasion for which the entire Zodiac was constructed; undoubtedly alludes to several extremely important rituals: as the rise of Sirius annually signalled the time of the Enthronement of the Pharoah. The Pharoah was Himself the Sun reborn as the Hawk and Sirius was His mother Ast, it is the stellar pattern commemorating an occasion of these rites of Union where the divine realm was able to manifest upon the Earth via its physical incarnation and double power was able to be channelled to Egypt via the Temple. The portrayal of this High Ritual and its participants is forever preserved within this magnificent Zodiac.From these perspectives it becomes clearer why the Zodiac is depicted as it is and also gives further insight into the Inner plans of the Temple layout of Egypt and the various temples flanking its banks may also be identified with the stars which are located on either side /around Draco.

With the importance of the interconnection between the three realms in mind, next follows a Rite aimed at making this a living reality, experienced within; the Temple being the mind and body of the practitioner.

Names & Images of the Stars Near the North Pole:

1.DRACO: the Hippopotamus Goddess Taur-t, also called Hesamut with an unnamed Crocodile upon Her back - this is possibly the Star Serpentaria.

2.URSA MAJOR: the Bull God Asar, also called Meskheti.

3.URSA MINOR: Heru, also called the Warrior An.

4.Two unnamed Men, one holding a spear with which he attacks a Crocodile.

5. An unnamed Hawk - possibly interpreted as the Pole Star, Polaris.

6.Serquet in woman -form.

7. A Lion.

8. A Crocodile Serisa.

Implicit within the use of the freedom to go forth by day and by night, is that we must fully incarnate the energies of Earth, our home, before seeking to commune in union with the energies of the Sky realm.

One way to approach Rites of Ascent, is to view them as a form of 'mirror' of Rites of Descent: as Journeying into the Tuat (the Western ancestral realm) brings each of us to an experience of the God (Asar)within and an experience of the depths of the subconscious, the Mysteries of the Night; we are engaged in a Journey to the inner regions of the earth itself. Likewise, Journeys into the Celestial Realms has the potential to bring each one into a conscious perception of the elevated consciousness which exists within the Mysteries of the Night, when approached from a different direction, or perspective, that of the outer regions of our Solar System.

This ancient fact that *both ascending and descending relate to the night* is worthy of a deep and prolonged contemplation before embarking upon either Rite. These undeniable links between the Stellar Realm and the Tuat is one explanation of why Lord Anpu is a Godform aligned to both a Star (Sep-t, or Sirius) as well as being the Opener of the Ways which lead to the Tuat, wherein He acts as a trustworthy Guide and Guardian.

In this alignment of the Night-Sky and the Tuat, understandable in one way in terms of the Daily and Nightly Journeys of the Sun and by experiencing both realms from the familiar 'launching pad' of Earth, we are able to awaken our inner potential in a balanced manner.

It is vital to remember that the Sun has both a Daily (Light) and Nightly (Dark) aspect and that the primary underlying reason behind all ancient Egyptian Rites is to effect a safe renewal of the Solar power. This is a pattern which we each may partake in, for our consciousness also has a Light (khu) and a Dark, or Shadow (khaibit) aspect. This fundamental balance and interplay between aspects and realms is affirmed in many different ways within the ancient Egyptian Tradition and that both aspects are necessary to the success of the process of renewal. Another example of this is in the pairing or 'Twinning' of a Light aspect of a neter with its Dark aspect: Ast /Neb-t het; Heru /Anpu; Nekhbet/Uadjet; Asar/Set; Het-heru /Sekhmet /Bast.

Reflect on the above: all along both human and neter exemplify the same patterns. Ultimately, it is through the intimate interrelationship between Above and Below that we come to an experience and an inner knowing of our self as divine.

There are many ways to approach Rites of Ascent, the following are offered as a means to stimulate your own personal awakening to this realm:

> 1. Enact a Ritual Journey to each of the Seven Planets as a means of establishing a sympathy with the Journey into the Tuat, which involves Seven Doors.

> 2. Journey to individual stars one at a time, to learn their lessons; in this we always seek to manifest their light upon the Earth.

3. Ceremonially experience the Day Sky in comparison to the Night-Sky.

Each of these Journeys requires that we have a vehicle; within the ancient Egyptian lore even the Sun required a boat to move safely both Above and Below; our consciousness is no different.

Amongst Ast's most sacred ritual objects is a Boat-Shaped Vessel of Gold, which enables an intimate experience of the Goddess' power.

By constructing a spiritual 'boat of gold' around us, that is, our own light-body sahu and khu consciously extended at will; whilst invisible in the outer is clearly delineated upon the inner planes. This may be accomplished through use of inner sight and ritual gesture; our inner vision of our sahu and khu extended outward upon the inner planes (i.e astral). Though the physical body may remain where it is upon the Earth, our sahu accompanied by ba, ka and khu carry our conscious-ness into the Stellar Realms. This may have been already experienced, without conscious direction, at the point of falling asleep and after during dreams, particularly those involving flight - for our spiritual and light-bodies do fly upward and outward into the vast Sky regions of Nut, from where they originated.

For those experienced in certain other types of Pathworkings, you will notice a particular difference, in that the Tracks/Paths which are walked in Pathworkings are absent from this Egyptian Journey, where you must navigate your consciousness as contained within the spiritual and light-bodies as it ascends and descends through trackless regions. This is one reason why a 'boat 'accompanied by suitable Guardian figures is an important part of the Rite.: even Ast's 'Boat-Shaped Vessel of Gold' had a Guardian figure of a Cobra sculpted upon its handle, hood flared over it.

Refer to the Hieroglyphic Forms of Ast and also the various Gods and Goddesses who are intrinsic to the outplaying of Her lore and it becomes apparent that certain forms are powerfully suited to accompanying a Stellar Journey; some examples of this are: Lord Anpu; a Winged Serpent; Bird-aspects of both Gods and Goddesses.

Hours of the am Tuat (Night) Particularly Suited to Stellar Rites:

- To Commence a Journey: immediately after Sunset and not later than 7 p.m.

- To Ascend (Go Forth By Night): mid-evening 7-10 p.m (complete before 11p.m.)

- To Explore Deep Space: between the hours of 1-4 a.m. (commence after 1.am.).

- To Return (Go Forth By Day): 4 a.m. and completed prior to, or at Sunrise.

Keeping in mind that there are Twelve Hours of the Night in which to Journey; it will be apparent that this, in effect, time-tracks all the hours of the am Tuat and follows the movement of the celestial bodies across the heavens and also gives a clear indication as to which times are better for particular Stars:

- Rising Stars: after Sunset to mid-evening, in the East.

- Setting Stars: the hours immediately prior to Sunrise, in the West

- Circumpolar Stars (i.e those which never 'rise' or 'set') the three pivotal hours of 11 p.m - Midnight - 1 a.m;

with Polaris at Midnight exactly; once a link has been made with these Stars they may be attuned to on a different level during their 'invisible' period during the Day Hours of 11 a.m - Midday - 1 p.m.

Rítual to the Místress of the Stars

Preliminary Preparations:

1. Obtain an Astronomical map of the Night-Sky in your Hemisphere.

2. Calculate when/if Key Stars such as Sep-t, Antares,Draco, Polaris etc are visible where you dwell.

3. Calculate which Day, during their visible period, is the most appropriate to undertake this Rite.

4. The Dark and New Moon Phases, before it becomes visible are best for viewing the Stars; whilst the time of New Moon is suited to Journeying.

5. Prior to this Rite, attune yourself to the Star you have selected when and whilst it is visible, when it Rises, for a period of not less than Seven nights. (Keep Record of any dreams during this period). When working with Sep-t, increase this to Eleven nights.

At the Hour Best Suited to the Star You Have Chosen enter the Shrine after bathing and robing in the white linen and clothed with the appropriate attitude of devotion and the heartfelt seeking of the Gift of Stellar illumination.

Candle -White only; Incense - Star Anise only.

Place the solitary candle upon the Altar (unlit) and perform the Shrine Opening (Chapter.4); when you reach the part where you intone Anpu, Light the candle and burn a large quantity of Star Anise. At the point when you would invoke Sep-t, trace the Sign of the Star you are seeking to the East, Above and over the Altar using the smoke of the Censor.

Raise the Wand of Power and trace the Sign of the Star and seeing this Sign brilliantly illuminated above where you stand, intone (pronounce, vibrate) the name of the Star and as you intone this, draw the Starlight down and touch your brow, heart, genitals and feet; as the light reaches your feet say:

I, (pronounce your name) am a Being of Light and have entered into the Holy Place with a pure heart; I adore the Light which shines forth from within the body of Nut Queen of the Night, Mother of Ast, Mistress of the Stars, grant favour, that even I a (state Child/Devotee/Priestess/Priest etc) *may come to know you and within thy embrace travel, upon your limbs and hair, that I may visit the Stellar regions of the night from where I came - for therein burns the eternal flame of all that is divine; source of the Elder Powers, I seek favour upon this Journey, that I may bring into my life* (state your objective) *and a true knowledge of my highest self, that I may better serve the purpose for which I am here.*

Ancient and eternal, sacred light; birthplace of the neter which we have come to know and see; we are all Children of Nut, but you who are the dwelling place of the race of Egypt, grant that I may be illumined with a portion of thy ancestral light.

Using the Wand of Power, trace around yourself Ast's 'Boat of Gold' and accompanied by your Guardian/Guide/s, ascend towards the Star you have invoked.

Alternately, if you do not wish to ascend; see the Star's Light shine in a brilliant shaft through to where you stand and then assume the glyphic representation of a Star: arms and legs outspread. In this position, draw the Light down into your body and through all your limbs until it reaches your feet and the Earth whereon you stand.

Offer the prayer:

> *May I be a worthy receptacle of this Holy Light,*
> *May* (name the Star) *be manifest within my life.*

Become open to experiencing how the Stellar Light may work within/through you and for what purpose; this may come as a vision, a sensation, a thought even a feeling; remember. Change body posture into an honouring stance (body upright hands raised to heart level, palms facing outward), pause then make Offerings.

If Journeying within the Boat, keep focused on your destination by saying:

> *Upon the Body of Nut*
> *May I be transported*
> *Safely and swiftly*
> *To the home of* (name Star).

At any point you may return in the reverse of how you came, this is essential if you become vague, faint, or unclear.

With consciousness maintained, continue to focus upon the Star until you arrive. Experience its Wisdom; Remember and return in the reverse of how you arrived.

When you have ensured that you have really 'returned' - see your boat descend and land upon Earth, disembark, thank your Guardian/Guide/s and then reabsorb the light of the boat within your sahu and khu and make suitable Offerings.

To Conclude Say:

May my khat ever be united with my sahu
That I may Journey to places hidden
May my ab be united with my ba
That the Journey be accomplished safely
May my ka accompany me that each Journey be blessed
with Wisdom
May each Journey energise both mykhu and khaibit
That I May Shine forth a balanced Light to Guide my
life and
Quest to become un-nefer.

Perform the *tua-shen-taui* gestures of the Shrine Opening and bringing hands and feet together at Heart level, bow your head towards the Altar in respect and Thanks and Record your experiences.

Careful study and contemplation of the ancient lore surrounding the Rise of Sep-t, will also give guidance into other appropriate uses/orientations of a Rite of Ascent.

As the Stellar Houses of the eternal flame of divinity, Stellar Rites should always be approached with absolute respect, reverence and child-like wonder, for they are a a Gift from neter.

As has been explained elsewhere within this book, there is a complex lore surrounding the Jackal-headed Lord Anpu and His ancient connection the Ast's Stellar Birthplace, Sep-t (Sirius). It is true that to obtain both entry and safety within both the realms of Ascent and Descent, that a real relationship with Lord Anpu be both developed and maintained. This can be initiated through the consecration of a Statue of the God which becomes a focus of adoration and which, becoming easily visualized, serves a focus of guidance between worlds. There is another form of stellar journey which may be potently undertaken within the Egyptian system and one which is also recognizable within the scheme of the holy Tree of Life of the Kabbala. This journey is not to be undertaken without, perhaps, many years of preparation - for there is the real and absolute danger of getting lost if success was obtained in getting out into these realms prematurely.

Performing a Ritual to the Mistress of the Stars provides a means to gain a familiarity with the Stellar regions in a directed manner, for the starting and ending location are always known. Once familiar,certain key points outlined may be utilized to become a Ritual to Open the Way. It will be apparent to the practitioner who has spent much time and devotion in understanding these Mysteries and who has also accomplished many Rites of Ascent and Descent, how to gain access to the hidden places. For it is very true of these ancient realms that what can be told and what is seen and known is much less than what remains invisible.The power within these invisible abodes is also of an increasing potency. However, though hidden from view, the keys to gain access to such places have always been available and it is a logical part of this journey that each one, in their own time and when they are ready, find their own way into these places through their own effort - this has ever been the way. There are other practicalities of mind to consider, for without the appropriate preparation, there are real dangers to the mind in venturing out into trackless abodes.

In all these matters, Lord Anpu is ultimately the Godform who grants access to these realms -for He is Lord of the Western Horizon in the same manner that His brother Heru is Lord of the Eastern Horizon. Let Him then be appropriately honoured in the quest to unlock the ancient gate.

10.

Rite of Descent

As the Sun descends towards the West at Sunset, the potential for a further journey arises. Here in the Western region, the Immeasurable Abode, the full potency of the Egyptian system for renewal and perpetuation is expressed through the nightly Journey of The Sun in the Solar Boat, overcoming many perils, to rise renewed in the East the following Dawn. It is here, in the West, that Ast's beloved Asar dwells and it is from here that He returns as the Child Heru.

Of all the aspects of the Egyptian religion, it is this region which has been most ignored; the description of the beings who dwell here are often fearsome and inspire avoidance. However, understanding the importance of this region to and what it represents, makes it equally worthy of study, respect and to experience.In the previous chapter we have worked with the sky and stellar realms of the East and have experienced ascent, light,heat, fire and the moisture of the incoming Inundation. Now the realm which exists to the West must be explored; this will lead us to an experience of descent, absence of light, cold, dryness and yet also an inner light, a dark flame. As the experience of ascent takes us into the stellar regions and can be called a journey into outer space, so the descent into the Western ancestral region the Tuat, becomes a journey within - to the depths of our individual psyche, our own inner space.

The reason that the Egyptian Tuat can also be explained and experienced as a dimension within our own minds, can be made understandable through the correlation of the daily and nightly journey of the Sun, with the parallel journey that our individual consciousness makes each day. We rise in the morning when we awake, we journey through our day's activities in much the same manner as the Sun travels across the sky, we set in the evening when we sink into the 'Western Region' of the subconscious and sleep and like the Sun itself, our consciousness continues to journey and explore the vast and deep in the form of dreams and astral journeys and like the Tuat itself, our subconscious life can have its fair share of suppressed fearsome creatures and even nightmare imagery.

When approached in this manner, the Tuat becomes a much more accessible land and one that it can be seen that we actually travel to, each night in a subjective fashion and here in this ancestral region, our own ancestors dwell. In the Egyptian Tuat, the region that we also will explore objectively, the Great Ancestor God Asar (Osiris) rules as King of the Dead and it is to here that Ast journeys to enable the birth of Heru. As Ast is so beloved of Asar both She and Her loyal followers are permitted to travel here and to return safely.

This Journey of Descent is in all manners parallel to the Journey into the Otherworld made by Inanna-through a series of seven steps- to resurrect Tammuz in the Sumerian ritual cycle and also may be understood in terms of the Journey into the Otherworld made by Arthur, accompanied by sister-enchantress Morgan, within the Celtic lore. These comparisons are made to assist the awareness of modern practitioners that this Journey of Descent is an ancient and universally experienced pattern which holds the seeds of immense initiatory power. An understanding of the full range and dynamics of Isis' capabilities is impossible without fully acknowledging Her Sovereign domain within the Egyptian Otherworld. The number seven also emerges within the Tuat as a key; for it is through gaining admission to an inter-connected series of seven Arits or palace-fortresses, that Ast eventually enters into the direct presence of Her beloved Asar. Likewise Her followers, must also gain admission via the Doors of the seven Arits, in the quest to obtain the self-knowledge that only a direct encounter and experience of death - whilst alive - can provide.

This of course is partly the reason why the Journey itself remains so unknown and yet paradoxically, so feared. But let not Her followers fear that in this vital quest that they are alone ! Just as the Goddess Ast Herself was accompanied into the Tuat-regions by the Jackal-headed Lord of the necropolis, Anpu (Anubis), so too, may we invoke for His aid and guidance as we descend. Lord Anpu emerges as one of the most beneficent guardian and protective God-forms within the Egyptian system that we may be blessed to have as our companion. Lord Anpu's potent connection with the Otherworldly regions has its source in the following: as the firstborn son of Osiris and Isis' own sister, Nepthys; Anpu is the heir to Osiris' Throne in Amen-t. That Anpu is the firstborn of Osiris whilst still alive and King of Egypt and not Heru - who was not born until after Osiris' murder, has already been discussed in an earlier chapter. The implications of this are profound and may cause surprise to some. However, the union of Nepthys (Egy: Nebt-het) and Osiris without Isis' prior knowledge, is well-documented within Egyptian religious texts. The subsequent adoption of Anpu by Ast after Her husband's murder attests to Her love and loyalty of the God - for at that stage Anpu was Osiris' only child; Ast not conceiving until Asar was well and truly dead.

But what does this all really mean? On one level, the inter-action of the various gods and goddesses can be interpreted in terms of natural phenomena and the sequence of day and night. Within this eternal pattern, Ast is the Dawn air, or Dawn sky, upon and within which the new-son/sun Heru rises daily; Her twin and sister, Neb-t-het represents the night-sky air of the pre-dawn hours, whilst Asar is both the hidden sun of the night hours. The union of the hidden, or black sun, with the night sky produces an awareness of the vastness of outer space and where day and night meet; this threshold dweller, the Horizon,whom we have profound awareness of at dusk and dawn is Lord Anubis. This pattern reveals the reasons in nature, of why Asar 'had' to be dead before the son born of His legitimate wife Ast - Heru - could be born; for if the father never descended into the Western regions there could be no son. The Sun would never move from its place in the sky. This has important parallels for us in making our Journey, for the Sun is also our consciousness, which must be renewed, we too must raise our inner sun-child to great heights.

The Jackal-headed Lord has the ability to Open the Ways for us, in a sense He is the key-holder of the hidden-door of the horizon, which opens briefly and with great purpose at dusk and dawn to allow the sun to both descend and to rise again. It is suggested that a statue of Anubis be appropriately cleansed and consecrated and installed in the room where one sleeps at night and purposefully invoked in the Shrine, as an ongoing work to maintain contact with the consciousness of these realms both prior to the initial Journey being made and also once contact has been established. Anpu creates a beneficent and highly-protective atmosphere in a room, when properly acknowledged.

His energy can often be perceived in terms of a youthful companion, both playful and yet holding the immense secrets of the hours of the night. In this connection, it is fitting to remember, that Ast's own stellar birthplace - Sirius - is often spoken of in terms such as Dog-star and whilst Anpu is a Jackal, the hunting, guiding, guarding, alertness and companionship abilities of dogs provide a readily accessible insight into the qualities of Anpu; keeping in mind that the Jackal is a wild and undomesticated scavenger. However, Ast

Herself was always in the company of either loyal Lord Anpu, or dogs and in many magical works He becomes Her partner replacing Asar.

The connection to Sirius provides a stellar gateway and this may be located kabbalistically at the Eleventh sphere of the Otz Chiim, Daath, or Knowledge; for it is knowledge of the Otherworld, which in all cultures, completes the mystery-cycle. Daath itself is positioned as an invisible gateway upon the 'horizon-line' which is formed when the invisible line of the Abyss is drawn between Chokmah and Binah. In this, Anubis' position as first-born is illustrated, for Chokmah (Father) and Binah (Mother) lay immediately above Daath; whilst Tiphareth, the sphere of the Sun and Heru lays directly beneath. Awareness of this stellar-key to the sphere of Daath provides a first link in shifting consciousness from the apparent worlds of the preceding sephiroth and provides the dual role of both launching our consciousness into the night-sky stellar regions and also enables us to descend within to the most inner regions of that star-space within our minds. Linking our individual consciousness to a stellar vehicle provides the means to cross the trackless abode of the vast Night-Sky region of Ascent whilst incarnate: these are journeys out into the imageless archetypal realms. In contrast, a Descent into the Tuat will lead you via a well-signposted and tracked journey, into a realm of archetypal images.

The Way and the Work being thus prefigured and dynamically illustrated within the ancient Egyptian religion, it is for us today to make our way into these regions and to return with great clarity of purpose and a renewal of life. No two Journeys can or ever will be the same; we each have our own adversaries to meet and to conquer and our own wisdom to obtain and though the path has been plainly laid out within the ancient texts, we may still pause before, or perhaps even refrain from undertaking this Journey.

What follows is a rite of descent into the Tuat (27b). Do not enter here frivolously or without preparation and respect for it is the abode of the eternally living Egyptian gods.

Ritual of Gaining Admission Into the Tuat

Having performed the preparations of both establishing and maintaining the Shrine and Temple and being familiar with these powers and the means by which they are called forth and having earnestly sought the favour of the ancient Ones and been granted an awareness of how to proceed; it will become clear to each Initiate when to undertake this Ritual. This is not for those who have either just entered the Temple or who have not as yet attained at least unto a priestly Grade possessing understanding.

Choose a Day and Hour suited to this work, according to your intuition and Guidance and ever keep in mind that it is into the Realm of both the Night and the deep that you venture.Seven are the Doors by which you will descend into the Night and Seven are the trials by which you must pass by the Doorkeepers; ever-Watchful are they who wait at the Gates of Power and ever-vigilant must you be in your Descent.

Prepare the Temple as for a Ritual of the highest importance and carefully Invoke and Awaken the Powers you choose to accompany you on your Descent. In all things, use absolute clarity of mind and focus of intention. Mark well the ur heka by which you will gain access to these places.

Using the Wand of Power to the East, above and over the Altar, trace *ankh, tjed, uas*. Turn Sunwise to the West and see an immense Gateway surrounding a Door, atop which these three signs of power brilliantly shine.

Before each of the Seven Doors you will encounter Three Guardians perhaps of fearful sight; do not hesitate in the utterance of the ur heka and know that these Guardians will either Admit you or turn you away depending upon what they See within your Heart. Once admitted, allow time to experience what is within each of these abodes and remember that you may accurately record what is seen upon your return.

Door #1 pronounce *BySekhet-her-asht-aru by Smetti* and *by Hakheru I, the Asar* (pronounce you own name) *come to this place, I revere and worship all the powers of the deep and you Asar, lead me to you Abode. Let me not hear the hated words or the names which bring destruction; for you Asar live and move by your own power through both the heavens and the worlds below. I am Judged in the Hall of Truth and found to be True, in my body of light I come to you, Lord Anpu Guide me into the places unknown that I may See the God.*

Door #2 pronounce *ByUnhat bySeqt-her* and *byUst I, the Asar* (pronounce your own name) *come with Truth in my mouth and acknowledge that the Gods of Truth are hidden in the depths; to Lord Tehuti do I offer up the pure offerings that He may lead me forward. May I be permitted to within these regions unknown and may I see the God.*

Door #3 pronounce *By Unem-hauatu-ent-pehui by Seres -her* and *by Aa I, the Asar* (pronounce your own name) *come with Truth in my mouth and in the depths of this place proclaim that I am the One who Judges right from wrong what is repulsive to the God exists not here and I adore the powers of the deep with pure offerings I have discovered the hidden paths of power to renew the God so lead me on.*

Door #4 pronounce *By Khesefherasht-kheru by Serestepu* and *byKhesef-at I, the Asar* (pronounce your own name) *come with Truth in my mouth and say for all to hear that I have become the Child of the God and having ventured into the hours of the Night as His Child I say lead me to the God, for having come this far, I am worthy of being received into His presence.*

Door#5 pronounce *By Ankhfemfent byShabu* and *byTebherkehakheft I, the Asar* (pronounce your own name) *come with Truth in my mouth and say the bones of the God have been gathered and preserved, I am now the ancient One and having persevered and walked the hidden tracks, may I see the God.*

Door#6 pronounce *By Atek-tau-kehak-kheru by An-her* and by *Ates-her-ari-she* I, the Asar (pronounce your own name) *come with Truth in my mouth and say that even I have become a god and Opened the Hidden paths, Lord Anpu you go before me and create new tracks, I know the ur heka and as Child of the God I defend His name and have been Crowned as a justified one in the places of the ancestors now take me to the God.*

Door#7 pronounce *By Sekhmet-em-tesu-sen by Aa-maa-heru* and *byKhesefkhemi I, the Asar* (pronounce your own name) *come with Truth in my mouth being made pure of all the things which you detest, I salute you ancient One ! I have advanced amongst the Hidden Ways and the Way has been Opened for me; I am of the Aset Shemsu and as the Goddess descended into the depths to be reunited with Her Beloved, so even I have come in this way to worship the God in His secret place.*

If Admission has been Gained through all Seven preliminary Doors, wonders will be seen, for you will be Granted Admission into the Living presence of Asar Himself, where He dwells as King of the Tuat; the dwelling of the God is amongst and protected by Ten Pillars of Divine Light, so take care that you enter there with absolute respect.

The Ritual is concluded in precisely the reverse order to which you entered and take care! that you exit through each Door in the correct order and that you close each door behind you. Make appropriate offerings. *Ankh-tjed-uas.*

Certain points should be made regarding this Ritual:

Whether male or female, ultimately we are all and will all become, the 'Asar...' This is the underlying and foundation belief essential to understanding the deeper recesses of power within the ancient Egyptian system. Without becoming the God, it would be impossible to traverse these realms and achieving a renewal of life. This is both a literal renewal whilst in life and also the future promise of resurrection after death.. Ultimately, all spells, all magicks, all words and rites of power have as the subliminal and often literal aim of achieving this purpose. Every offering and hymn of praise, ultimately seek to obtain the favour of the ancient and mighty Ones who are in possession of the keys of power by which this renewal is effected. The works we accomplish, in life,within the Temple of Ast, have as their purpose this same underlying motive. Every time we offer praise and sustenance to the Goddess and every time we renew the power of the Shrine we are also, in effect, renewing the power of the Shrine of our own lives.

It cannot be emphasised enough, that ultimately, there is nothing 'exterior' or 'remote' about the ancient Egyptian rites, for this Temple is alive within the mind and body of every practitioner who seeks to renew the life of the Shrine. By enacting a Ritual Journey such as this, we are also acknowledging the life and power of the Ancestral Realm and in effect, re-affirming our own kinship with both this realm and our own ancestors. The appropriateness and in fact, the necessity of both acknowledging and ritualizing this kinship lays in the ability of the ancestors and the ancestral realms to effect changes of immense benefit and potency in our lives.

Ceremonially honouring one's own ancestors is a prominent feature of the Ritual calendars of all ancient cultures, including the Celtic Tradition - from which many practitioners of the Western Mysteries, who also work with the Egyptian Mysteries - are descended (i.e. the October 31st -November 1st, Samhuinn or Samhain Celebration).

For this reason alone, performing a Tuat Journey should be viewed as another means of approaching and paying our respects to the ancestors - the Egyptian Gods and Goddesses ultimately being seen and understood as the Divine ancestors; for it is absolutely true that all who come within the Egyptian Temple, being reborn as Initiates, at that time also become Children of the Gods.

Having built the Temple anew and renewed its power through Daily and Annual Rites; having learnt of the ancient identity and powers of the Goddess and perhaps even having accomplished the great work of uniting our life and mind with the eternal life of the God within His palace, we come to rest and reflect upon the fact which remains - that we have undertaken and continue to undertake all these works as humans ever striving to become Asar un-nefer, that is, perfected. To this end, it should be the dedication of every aspirant who enters the Temple, that their every work and expression of will should reflect and be in harmony with this lofty and Divine Purpose.

Let then, this quest for perfection spread out its blessing far and wide, that our devotions within the Temple not become a remote and meaningless thing, but as in Egypt, may our work in some small way contribute to the renewal of the life of the society and time which we each live within and surely, there can be no greater or more worthwhile manifestation of these ancient mysteries than to aspire to having success in this aim.

11.

Poweʀ of the Ages

"There is in everyone 'divine power' existing in a latent condition... This is one power divided above and below; generating itself, making itself grow, seeking itself, finding itself, being mother of itself, father of itself, daughter of itself, son of itself - mother, father, unity, being a source of the entire circle of existence"

Hippolytus, *"The Great Announcement"* (15)

The many facets of Ast's ancient identity having been revealed to contain a wholeness and creative force seemingly 'hidden' for many centuries and re-surfacing in modern times, leads to consideration of Her role in current and future times. As years have numbers and days have names, so one way the passage and progress of time throughout the ages has been marked is by the acknowledgement that Earth's development has been under the auspices of the divine and that the predominant energy of each time period is governed by a god/goddess form embodying the astrological force of that time. From the Greek does the notion of an 'Aeon' derive; each Aeon being reckoned to take several thousand years to unfold and then to give way to the next power.

This unfolding of power through time is often called the Succession of the Aeons, or Aeonic Succession and has been often depicted as a lineal occurrence; that is, one Aeon concludes before the next one commences. With advances in our understanding of time itself and the notion that parallel worlds and time-periods exist, the portrayal of the Aeons can quite legitimately be reconsidered to encompass this view. In this final chapter, this view of Parallel Aeons will be explored, with particular reference to the Egyptian powers which each Aeon is imbued and with an insight into how this view of Aeonic Succession as parallel domains of power is supported by an investigation of both the sacred Tetragrammaton of Kabbalah and through the hieroglyphs themselves.

Within the Holy Kabbalah and its glyphic representation the Otz Chiim, or Tree of Life, the patterns of creative energy are revealed as parallel dimensions or worlds being four in number - the Atziluthic (Divine, Creative); the Briatic (Archetypal, Archangelic); The Yetziratic (Formative, Angelic, Astral) and the Assiatic (Material, Manifest Existence).

It is within these worlds that all that is and all that will be is conceived, formulated and finally brought forth. One level, of necessity, reflects the power of the preceding or succeeding level; this however is a continuous cycle and in the interaction and flow of force to form a circuit is created, each realm being essential to the progressive unfolding of the next. This unfolding is both lineal and parallel in operation, in the apparent sense that all worlds function as both hermetic realms of immense power and yet, in the continuous interaction that is evident, they must also exist as parallel planes - all functioning simultaneously. It is within this pattern that the entire progress and function of the Tree works; each of the sephiroth (= 'number') also both progressively and simultaneously revealing aspects of existence. To each of the ten sephira are ascribed particular attributes,with sephiroth #1 Kether, being the absolute divine light which is progressively brought into a solid manifestation in sephiroth #10. Of particular importance to the unfolding of power through the ages are those sephira directly related to the archetypal patterns of the father (Chokmah #2) and the mother (Binah #3),being renewed through the manifestation of the son (Tiphareth #6) and the daughter (Malkuth #10).

These four sephira hold immense power. As has been noted in an earlier chapter, Ast, or Isis, has long been associated with the forces represented as emanating from the third sephiroth, Binah. Within Binah, the forces of time find their expression through the divine image of the Elder Mother, the Black Queen; who is at the same time both bright (fertile) and dark (sterile). The interplay between the tenth sephiroth, Malkuth and the third sephiroth, Binah provides one key to understanding this paradox; for one of the primary symbols of Binah Is the Throne; which is both the ideogram of Ast's (Isis) name and the translation of the Hebrew powers attendant upon that sphere, the aralim ('Thrones'). Similarly, Malkuth is imaged as a young and beautiful princess, a virgin, seated upon another Throne - She is the mother reborn in the form of the daughter, or if looked at from another angle, the daughter who will in time ascend the Throne becoming the mother.

The counterchange between the light and the dark aspects of the Goddess are experienced also in the relationship between Ast and Her twin sister Neb-t het (Nepthys).In one sense Isis and Nepthys are two aspects of one Goddess, in the same way that the mother and daughter represent two aspects of the same force. As Isis is the East, so Nepthys is the West. They are the two horizons which join above and below; one Goddess is the dawn and morning, the other the dusk and the dark of night.Each forms a complementary to its twin.

Apart from Her manifestation within the sphere of Binah, Isis is also associated with other sephira, the most often utilised are:

KETHER: Imageless and aspectless.

CHOKMAH: Uadjet; Ast uraeus.

BINAH: Ast; Nekhbet; Ast ur-t mut neter; Ast enth hem-t nesu; Neter mut.

(DAATH): Ast Anpu; Ast Septit; Neb-t aakhu; Ast Ament-t; Ast netchit.

CHESED : Ast-Maat.

GEBURAH: Ast ta -uh; Selket; Serket; Tabityt; Sekhmet.

TIPHARETH: Ast au ab; Ast aab-s Het-her; Het-heru; Me-hurit; Ast-Rait-set;Sekhmet.

NETZACH: Het-heru; Me -hurit; Ba-en-Ast (Bast);

HOD: Ast netrit-em renus-nebu; Maat; Urit hekau.

YESOD: Taur-t Ast; Bast.

MALKUTH: Ast em neb-t ankh; Ast sekhem em ankh neter; Ast uab.

(see Chapter 2: "Transformations" for elucidation of these aspects).

In addition to this, Ast is intimately related to the experiences of the following pathways - the astrological association of each pathway giving one key as to which of the above aspects are appropriate to utilise. These aspects may be usefully employed as an alternative goddess-form for pathworking to enable a continuity of the Egyptian mysteries:

GIMEL: The Priestess (Atu #2) Luna.

DALETH: The Empress (Atu #3) Venus.
ZAIN: The Lovers (Atu # 6) Gemini / Mercury.

YOD: The Hermit (Atu # 9) Virgo/Mercury.

LAMED: Justice (Atu # 11) Libra/Venus.

SAMEKH: Art (Atu # 14) Sagittarius/Jupiter.

TZADDI: The Star (Atu # 17) Aquarius/Uranus.

QOPH: The Moon (Atu # 18).

RESH: The Sun (Atu # 19).

SHIN: The Aeon (Atu # 20).

TAV: Judgement (Atu #21).

In this way it is seen that the power of the mother, Isis, extends throughout all worlds and numerous areas of the Tree Of Life. Returning to the fourfold pattern which is the basis of that Tree, its energy is also represented by the sacred four letters known as the Tetragrammaton YodHehVauHeh (YHWH) - with the father being the letter Yod, the mother being the letter Heh, the son being the letter Vau and the daughter being the letter Heh (final). it is in this sequence that the Aeonic Succession is meant to be prefigured; however difficulties arise with this overlay, due to the acknowledgement that the cycle of the mother Isis (Age of Taurus, times of ancient Egypt and Sumeria) preceded the age of the son Horus (Age of Aries, time of ancient Greece and Rome); then an obvious displacement of the daughter as history follows on to the Aeon of the father Osiris (Age of Pisces, time of history from Rome to the recent era) and then as portrayed widely throughout modern times, we are now in the time of the son again, with the Age of Aquarius arising. Apart from the obvious banishment of one quarter of the Tetragrammaton - the time or aeon of the daughter - it is also obvious that this historical unfolding of the Aeons does not fit the position of the letters of the Tetragrammaton as anciently used and reverenced; to convey this historical and astrological sequence the letters would have to be placed in the format HehVauYodVau.This of course is an extremely difficult equation as it reduces the holy fourfold pattern of the Tree Of Life to a triplicity (and so by extension would have to remove one entire plane or world of existence) and at the same time prevents the renewal of the principle of the mother, who may now no longer be reborn in the form of the daughter.

It is in this theme of renewal that the underlying meaning of these cycles blossoms forth in its fullest manifestation - practitioners who engage in devoted work with the Tree over time, experience this also in all levels of their being as a deep psychic liberation. In keeping with the ancient Egyptian patterns, including the dual nature of the Lands and the Kingship; it is suggested that for the Egyptian goddess and godforms to function within the fourfold pattern of the Tetragrammaton, that there must be this concept of dual renewal in operation. Often the portrayal of the Tetragrammaton, as discussed above, is that the father receives renewal through the son and this is valid, apparent and necessary. However, the renewal of the female principle - the mother being reborn and renewed through the birth of the daughter - is both dismissed and overlooked. It is apparent that for one half of the pattern to function at its fullest, that the other half must also be called into operation. This dual renewal is not only a valid interpretation of the Tetragrammaton, it is fully in keeping with the Tree Of Life itself, the Egyptian Goddess and Godforms which have long been ascribed to its holy letters and the Aeons which are figured within its fourfold pattern. Apart from this, dual renewal makes sense - for of what use is the renewal of only one half of the pattern (the father), when the birth of the forms of renewal (the son, the daughter) are dependent upon the other half (the mother)?

That each component of the Tetragrammaton is as important as the next should be apparent, or it would not exist. Without the full comprehension of the meaning of dual renewal, the cycle can never be fully empowered; nor can it function to renew itself.It is only when all four sections of the Tetragrammaton are activated that either a lineal or a parallel succession of power can take place. Figuring the daughter back into Her rightful palace is the work that must now take place in this Age of Aquarius* (28) - the age of the androgyne figure, the twin, both male and female; not only is there room for Her Aeon to flourish, it must be flourishing, else the Aeon of the son must neither have arrived. Father and mother, son and daughter: Osiris and Isis; Horus and Maat - these ancient Ones are the patterns by which we achieve the renewal of the power of the ages and also that of our own life - for is not the Tree also a pattern of the individual?

The inclusion of Maat as the Egyptian Goddess in whose form the daughter arises, has ancient precedent; the Egyptians themselves figuring Her into the images of enthronement carved upon stelae. In these, as Isis is paired with Her lover and brother Osiris; so too is Maat paired with Her lover and brother Horus. The pairing of these principles ensures that the Throne, the great ancestral power which descends from the mother (Ast /Isis) as has also been previously discussed, finds an Eldest Daughter form in which to be reborn.Long has She awaited the rebirth of that Aeon and the time is now, with the changeover of the astrological ages; the transformation of the old into the new. It will be remembered that the succession of the ancient Egyptian Throne was through the eldest daughter (Ast Herself being the eldest daughter of Nut and Geb); thus the necessity of a subsequent eldest daughter to pass the Throne to. Maat fulfils this criterion, being an extremely ancient Goddess and daughter of Ra, who both preceded Nut (Ast's mother) and yet becomes portrayed as following Her. It is in this manner that the power of renewal as occurring within a parallel domain becomes apparent. This is also without confusion, remembering that the ancient Egyptian view was and is, an expansive and simultaneously multi-dimensional universe.

It is when the holy tetragrammaton is translated into a hieroglyphic model, that the implications of 'leaving the daughter out' become most obvious:

Yod -   Father - Osiris - hieroglyph of His name = Throne and Eye.

Heh -   Mother - Isis - hieroglyph of Her name = Throne.

Vau -   Son - Horus - hieroglyph of His name = Hawk.

Heh -   Daughter - hieroglyph of Her name = Feather; also the Scythe.

From the father does the son inherit the eye, also called the Eye of Horus and this includes its complex solar/sexual symbolism. the daughter on the other hand, coming as She does at the end of the sequence is fittingly portrayed within the hieroglyphs used to represent Her - that is, the Feather Of Truth and the Scythe, the Saturnian tool of reaping.

In this manner, the daughter becomes the karmic repository of all that has been reaped from the previous three cycles, if the view of the Aeons as lineal is adhered to and as such, She is well-equipped to be the Goddess in the Egyptian Judgement Hall whose Feather is weighed against the individual's heart, deciding whether one is Justified and may pass on to the Blessed Lands - or not. In the end all will be made to account to Her. That this is an enormous amount of power, a force that can only be ignored with dire consequences should be clear. The Tetragrammaton sequence also highlights that She contains within Herself the combined essences of the father, the mother and the son, a parthenogenic quintessence. Then the cycle would begin again.

However as has been noted, this lineal model does not accord with the historical and astrological sequence. If on the other hand, a parallel view is adopted, it can be seen how the vast power of the ages, whilst still accumulating within the final Heh, the daughter, also remains concurrently activated within all other three dimensions. This is a far more wholistic view and one which in turn, brings forth great hope: for the problems of past times need not be repeated over and over again in the Age Of Aquarius! Learning from the deficiencies inherent in times when either the power of the mother or the father is dominant; the current and future time shows forth the promise of all cycles being activated simultaneously in a harmonious and complementary order. This, it seems, is an underlying message and promise of the Age Of Aquarius - that the World (Malkuth, the daughter) will be blessed with the reconstruction of the ancient Temple (Tiphareth), wherein the mysteries of the mother and the father will be equally celebrated, with the resultant beneficence being radiated forth to all worlds

To Conclude: An ur heka Dedicated To Each One In Their Quest

Living Ones
Co-existent, co-eternal
Without beginning, without end
Mighty are the Hidden Powers
Renewed from time to time
Released upon the Living
By the Dead:

In your Heart is Light
Let this Light Shine
Be seen as bright and luminous
Speak Truth Divine

In the shadows are the footprints
Waiting, they go beside and before
Protection from all hidden dangers
Life is not like before

From Age to Age
The Power Grows

Now and then a flicker shines forth
But when the Power really flows -
What One can do -
Who knows?

May you, like Isis, go forth
In every place where
Your ka desires to be.

Notes

1a. BUDGE, E.A. *The Book Of The Dead* University Books Inc. U.S.A. 1984 ed.
Excerpt from the Pyramid Texts, as quoted on p. 78.

1. Du QUESNE, Terence *Jackal At The Shaman's Gate* Darengo Publications U.K. 1991. p.49.

2. TROY, Lana Patterns Of Queenship in Ancient Egyptian Myth and History Uppsala, Sweden 1986.
p. 69 (italics added).

3. TROY ibid. p.69.

4. BREASTED, James Development Of Religion and Thought In Ancient Egypt Harper and Row Pub. New York 1959. p. xix.

5. TROY P.O.Q. p.5.

6. ELIADE as quoted in P.O.Q. p.13.

7. TROY P. O.Q. p.34.

8. HINCKLEY Richard Allen Star Names Their Lore and Meaning Dover Publications Inc. New York 1963. pp.94,307,308,434,437.

9.BARUCQ, Andre et DAUMAS, Francois Hymns et Prieres de L'Egypte Ancienne Les Editions du Cerf Paris 1980. pp.456, 457. Translation by Akkadia Ford,1996.

10. Original praise-verse by Akkadia Ford ©1997.

11.TROY P.O.Q. p.70.

12. BARUCQ, ibid. "Chant cultuel a Hathor " #133, p.445. Translation Akkadia Ford, 1996.

13. Ptolemaic Text, *"The Songs of Isis and Nepthys"*.

14.This speech combines sentiments expressed throughout both the B.O.D. and also Ast's ancient Temple inscriptions, into a new form as used within contemporary Rites of Ast and is from the unpublished Ceremonies of the Temple of Ast Maat.

15.Hippolytus as quoted in P.O.Q. p.14.

16.BUDGE H.D. Volume 1 pp.482, 483.

17.The usage of the title hem-t neter is thoroughly discussed by TROY in P.O.Q.

18. BUDGE ibid.

19.HINCKLEY, Richard Allen *Star Names Their Lore and Meaning* Dover Publications New York 1963. p.205.

20. BUDGE H.D. Vol. 1&2.

21a & 21b. Original praise verses to the Two Ladies by Akkadia Ford ©1996.

22.BUDGE H.D. Vol.1 *"A List of Hieroglyphic Characters"*, Section XVIII,#11.

23.The source of this Ptolemaic fragment I have been unable to locate; an apology is therefore offered to that source and should a current copyright holder exist, please notify the Publisher so that this note may be amended and so that they will be acknowledged in any reprinted editions of this work.

24.BUDGE H.D. Vol.2 p.932 #295.

25.The hieroglyphic forms of Ast are wholly derived from BUDGE H.D. Vol 1 & 2 pp. 47-52; 80-81; 172-173; 358-359; 453; 962-967. The allocation of these forms to a realm (A), (E), (S), (T) and to a sephiroth are original, the opinions of this author and for the purposes of this book and it is not implied that such allocation either originates with, or is sanctioned by Budge's scholarship.

26.BUDGE H.D. pp. 386b, 388 a&b, 389.

27a. "Ritual to the Mistress of the Stars " and 27b "Ritual of Gaining Admission Into the Tuat" from the unpublished sesh sba en tem neter Ceremonies of the Temple of Ast Maat
and may NOT be reprinted without the prior written consent of the Temple of Ast Maat.95.

*28. With regard to the Tetragrammaton, it is of immense interest that the form widely used that of the Yod-Heh-Vau-Heh is ascribed to the Astrological Sign of Aries; whilst the Sign of Aquarius is accorded the different form of Heh-Yod-Vau-Heh. The rich symbolic and practical differences between these two forms should be apparent; as is the conclusion that the former version is not applicable to the Age of Aquarius. (these two versions of the Tetragrammaton are sourced from amongst twelve variations listed in the: *Z-5 Secret Teachings of the Golden Dawn Book 2* (1992) by Pat & Chris Zalewski pp.157-165). Whilst each form of the Tetragrammaton is being aligned to one of the Twelve Tribes of Israel in the context of the Z-5 Book; it cannot go unremarked how the form for the Sign of Aquarius also perhaps, inadvertedly, supports the foregoing discussion regarding the Aeon of the Daughter: as this sequence of the four Holy Letters is in the correct position acknowledged as a Creation Pattern utilized within the ancient Egyptian Temple: that of Mother-Father-Son-Daughter - then the cycle begins again with each portion capable of renewal.

Interestingly, the form of the Tetragrammaton, ascribed to the Astrological Sign of Leo:Heh Vau Yod Heh, fits exactly with our knowledge of the sequence of the astrological ages i.e from Taurus (Heh),to Aries(Vau),to Pisces (Yod) to the present Aquarius (Heh). As Aquarius and Leo represent Signs which form a duality, being opposite to each other and thus represent a balance, this form of the Tetragrammaton presents a duad energetically to the current age.

Bibliography

BARUCQ, Andre et Daumas, Francois *Hymns et Prieres de L' Egypte Ancienne* Les Editions Du Cerf Paris 1980.

BEIR, Ulli *The Return Of The Gods* Cambridge University Press Cambridge 1975.

BLEEKER, C.J. *Egyptian Festivals Enactments Of Religious Renewal* Leiden Pub. Netherlands 1967.

BREASTED, James Henry *Development Of Religion and Thought In Ancient Egypt* Harper and Row Publishers New York 1959.

BUDGE, E.A. *An Egyptian Hieroglyphic Dictionary* Vol. 1 & 2 Dover Publications Inc. U.S.A. 1978. (Abbreviation (abb.) H.D.)

BUDGE, E.A. *Egyptian Magic* Dover Publications Inc. New York 1971.

BUDGE, E.A. *The Book Of The Dead* University Books Inc. U.S.A. 1984 ed. (abb. B.O.D.)

BUDGE, E.A. *The Gods of The Egyptians* Methuen and Co. London 1904.

CERNY, Jaroslav *Ancient Egyptian Religion* Hutchinson's University Library London 1952.

DENNING, Melita and Phillips, Osbourne *The Triumph of The Light: The Magickal Philosophy* Book 4 Llewellyn Pub. U.S.A. 1978.

Du QUESNE, Terence *Jackal At The Shaman's Gate* Darengo Publications U.K. 1991.

FATUNMBI, Awo *Fa'Lokun Oshun - Ifa and The Spirit of The River* Original Publications New York 1993.

FAULKNER, Raymond O *An Ancient Egyptian Book Of Hours* Griffith Institute University Press Oxford 1958.

FAULKNER, Raymond O T*he Ancient Egyptian Coffin Texts* (Vol.2 Spells 355-787) Aris and Phillips Ltd. England 1977.

FAULKNER, Raymond O (Translation) and Goelet, Dr. Ogden (Introduction and Commentary) *The Egyptian Book of The Dead - The Book Of Going Forth By Day* Chronicle Books San Fransisco 1994.

GOFF, Beatrice L. *Symbols Of Ancient Egypt In The Late Period - The XXIst Dynasty* Mouton Pub. The Hague Netherlands 1979.

GLEASON, Judith *Oya - In Praise Of An African Goddess* Harper San Fransisco 1992.

HINCKLEY, Richard Allen *Star Names Their Lore and Meaning* Dover Publications Inc. New York 1963.

HOFFMEIR, James Karl *Sacred In The Vocabulary Of Ancient Egypt - The Term DSR With Special Reference To Dynasties 1-XX* Universitatsverlag Freiburg Sweiz Paulusdruckerei Freiburg Sweiz 1985.

IDOWU, E. Bolaji *African Traditional Religions* SCM Press Ltd. London 1973.

JOHNSON, Sally B. *The Cobra Goddess Of Ancient Egypt* Kegan Paul International London 1990.

PARRINDER, E.G. *African Traditional Religion* Hutchinson's University Library London 1954.

REICHARDT, E. Noel (M.D.) *The Significance of Ancient Religions* George Allen and Company Ltd. London 1912.

REYMOND E.A.E. *The Mythical Origin Of The Egyptian Temple* Manchester University Press England 1969.

SAUNERSON, Serge *The Priest Of Ancient Egypt* Grove Press Inc. New York 1960.

SELIGMAN, C.G. *Egypt and Negro Africa - A Study In Divine Kingship* Routledge and Sons Ltd. Great Britain 1934.

TROY, Lana *Patterns Of Queenship In Ancient Egyptian Myth and History* Uppsala Sweden 1986. (abb. P.O.Q.)

FELLOWSHIP OF ISIS
Clonegal Castle
Enniscorthy
 Southern Ireland.

TEMPLE OF AST MAAT
P.O. Box 92
Newtown
N.S.W. 2042
Australia.

For further information on participation in the Living Mysteries of the Goddess; please include a self-addressed stamped envelope, or an International reply Coupon (IRC) with all enquiries.

Author's Note

No-one who ventures forth into the terrain of Ancient Egypt goes alone; we have the accumulated work of countless predecessors upon which to build. Though often unacknowledged, it is due to the vast efforts of many - from unnamed Egyptian labourers who excavated the ancient sites, to the distinguished scholars who interpreted what was discovered, that we much of owe our knowledge. Perhaps, a flaw of the academic has been to express Egypt as a culture long past; whilst a mistake of many who seek Egypt's spiritual treasures, has been to accept anything presented with an Egyptian name as being anciently true, without searching for historical truth as revealed by the Egyptians within their texts and other monumental writings. That the ancient Egyptian religion was a learned and scholarly pursuit is true; that within this is housed spiritual realities of immense passion and insight, is equally true. In this light, maybe combining a rigorous scholarly discipline with spiritual devotion, will enable us to approach this high wisdom appropriately.

As a source of unending illumination, *The Book Of The Dead*, Translation by Sir E. A. Wallis Budge (1916); has been my constant companion since acquiring the 1984 Edition (Citadel Press). It is this Translation which is the source-text of all references: both indirect (such as outlining or summarising key concepts it contains) and also direct quotes specifically attributed to *The Book of The Dead* as Footnoted within this present volume; all material is used with the written permission of the Publisher - Carol Publishing Group (USA) and due thanks are given for this permission.

Additionally, I wish to highlight the groundbreaking 1986 work of Lana Troy, as contained within her outstanding research volume. It was a fortunate mishap of, what I thought was 'the wrong book' falling from a shelf in a public library, when attempting to locate something else, that turned out to be Troy's work. Deceptively housed in a plain blue cover, this book finally provided a rigorous, academically examined excavation of the answer to a simple question, posed by a previous Egyptologist 'What was the Role of the Wife of Pharoah?' - this question drops like a pin shattering ages-old silence within rooms, once inhabited and long-since avoided. The complex exploration of the answer to this question comprises her book and in simple terms, the answer is 'Isis IS each Queen'; a perfectly logical equation given that each successive Queen bore the incarnate God; but the implications of which, have remained quite inconspicuous amidst the glare of focus which the Kingly principle has received.

Troy's detailed investigation of the motifs of dual renewal within ancient Egyptian lore, firmly re-instates the principle of female renewal, to where it should have always been - visibly acknowledged beside motifs of male renewal. I am indebted to her work for providing a scholarly paradigm of ancient Egyptian views regarding this principle, for she offers an authentic translation which substantiates as historically valid, anciently known and utilized; the patterns of renewal presented as spiritual formulae at certain points within this book. It is because this key principle goes unmentioned time and time again within writings pertaining to Egypt that Troy becomes so important, for she provides an external source which verifies such formulae (and undoubtedly, where there is one, there must exist many more).

These ancient principles, restated and translated form a living pattern, reaffirming the Egyptian belief that transformation and renewal can be experienced by each living thing: human and nature, male and female, plant and animal, each possesses the prerequisite condition for attaining these things; that is, being aspects of the divine in manifestation.

Whilst Troy's scholarship is only referenced briefly within this book, her exposition provided a source of timely inspiration and verification, amidst a very parched terrain. For this reason I express my thanks. All readers keen to explore this matter from the historical and scholarly perspective she presents are encouraged to seek out her work (see Bibliography for full details).

Appendix

On the Role of Women in Official Religion in Ancient Egypt

In approaching an understanding of the role of women within the official religion of ancient Egypt, "the perception of the relationship between the dynamic of the cosmos and the life of the individual is a central theme..." [1] and one which provides the patterns of interrelationship between the male and female officiants and celebrants of the Egyptian Temple. Pre-eminent amongst these, are the roles which the Wife of the Pharoah assumed, in her complimentary aspect as the incarnation of the divine sister and queenly wife, the 'God's Wife' (hm.t ntr, hr.yt nst) (2) who begets the child and heir to the throne, Horus and an examination of the formulae of the 'Birth House' within the major Temples dedicated to both Hathor and Isis reveals how this role functioned as the nexus of the human and divine realms. Women functioned at all levels of the Temple service including: dancers and musician-priestesses (hn.ywt, sm'.ywt, mrt) (3); mourners(dr.ty) (4); Prophetesses and w'.bt priestesses of a higher rank; through to the highest level of participation in the official religion as Adorers of the God (dw3.yt) and High-priestesses in their own right, whose investiture was a state occasion and whose titulary varied throughout Dynastic history depending upon which Temple they served within. That women's role within the ancient Egyptian religion has often been less regarded or discussed than that of her male counterpart, speaks more of the personal interests or bias of past writers, than it does to an actual void in evidence of women's roles.

From the commencement of the historic period in Egyptian history, the mythical framework for the religion was initially centred around Heliopolis to the North and the religion of the Sun and the Stars and it was here that the first mound of creation was located. The creation legends of the divine Ennead of Heliopolis provided the eternal ancestral matrix (Osiris-Isis) from which the first historic royal brother-sister pairing emerged in Egypt and each ensuing Pharoah was regarded as an Incarnation of the first divine falcon Horus during his life, paradoxically wedded to his royal sister who represented both his mother and lover-wife (a composite of Hathor-Isis). Thus, the first and arguably, the pre-eminent role that any woman ever held within the ancient Egyptian religion was as the God's Wife (hm.t ntr):

"3st wr.t mw.t ntr nb.t 'Iw.rk
hm.t ntr dw3.t ntr dr.t ntr
mw.t ntr hm.t nsw wr.t
skr.t nb.t hkr.w 'ht
nb.t 3bw 3hht
'Imty mh 'h.t m nfr.w=s
'id.t 'ht hn.wt rsw.t
'ty.t gs.t m st ntr.yt
'igp. wrh 3ht m shd=s
srit bnr.t mrw.t hn.wt nt sm'w mhw
'ir.t md.w m hn.w psdt
ssm.tw hr st r=s
'ir.yt pt wr.t hs.wt nb.t i3m.t
hnms.t hn.t=s tftf m 'n.tyw w3d "

("O, Aset (i.e Isis) the Great, God's Mother, Lady of Philae
God's Wife, God's Adorer and God's Hand

God's Mother and Great Royal Spouse
Adornment and Lady of the Ornaments of the Palace

"Lady and desire of the green fields
Nursling who fills the palace with her beauty
Fragrance of the palace, Mistress of Joy,
Who completes her course in the divine place *
Rain-cloud that makes green the fields when it descends
Maiden sweet of love, Lady of Upper and Lower Egypt,
Who issues orders among the divine Ennead
According to whose command one rules
Princess, Great of Praise, Lady of Charm,
Whose face enjoys the trickling of fresh myrrh " [5]

It is to be noted, that amongst these epithets of Ast (Isis being the Greek translation of Her Egyptian name), several could equally be applied to Het-her (Hathor) and the priestesses who fulfiled various roles within the religion. Hathor was a Goddess intimately associated with the beautiful and bountiful aspects of life: music, dance, jewellry, perfumes and the "Fragrance of the Palace - Mistress of Joy", a possible allusion to the kalas, or 'perfumes' associated with the act of love itself. The interchange between these Goddesses also becomes increasingly obvious as we examine the role of the 'Wife of the God', that is, the Wife of the Incarnate God, the Pharoah and as the Wife of the divinity Himself.

A comparison with other inscriptions from both Ast's Temple at Philae and Het-her' Temple at Denderah reveals this to conceal the most important functions of the Royal 'Wife of the God', relating as it does to the Mysteries of the Birth House and the dual ceremonies attendant upon conception and delivery of the Sun, that were enacted therein. The inference contained within this, is that, each 'Wife of the God' was viewed as a direct incarnation of the Goddess upon the Earth and that during such ceremonies, both she and the Pharoah were imbued with the divine ancestral powers, in effect becoming the God and Goddess during the hiero-gamos.Without this shift in perception the incarnation of the Divine Horus upon Earth would have been impossible and the notion of a lineage of Divine Kingship over Egypt likewise becomes untenable.

Within this text is also a symbolic allusion to an aspect of the installation ceremony of the 'Wife of the God', who after being crowned and regaled with the jewellry and crown of the Goddess with whom she is identified, is "appointed Mistress of the whole circuit of the solar disk" (6a); that is, the one woman in the Two Lands who is able to "complete her course in the divine palace" * and one whose religious functions cover the full spectrum of the Solar cult, that is, she serves as High-Priestess of both the East (Sun -rise, birth of the royal heir) and the West (Sunset), High-Priestess of the mortuary cult and Chief Mourner; the one who gives rebirth to the Sun through the hours of the night. It is to be noted that a parallel exists with the Goddess Het-her' own titulary and functions, as symbolised through Her ideograms, which serve as both means of identification and as headdresses in context of the religion and its imagery. For Het-her, too, has an Office as nb-t 'Imn-t, the 'Lady of the West', the geographic location of the necropolis, in addition to Her role in the East each dawn. (7)

Theologically, there is an interchange between both the Goddess Het-her and Her earthly counterpart, the royal High-Priestess and hm-t ntr and the animal transformations of the Solar Cow and Cobra. As the 'Lady of the West'; and to fulfil her religious functions as the "Mistress of the whole circuit of the solar disk" (6b), an identification with the Cobra- Goddess nb-t skr, or mr.t skr ("She Who Loves Silence") forms a complementary aspect in the realm of death, to the Celestial Cow who daily gives birth to the Sun in the East. The relation of the Divine Cobra to the female principle within ancient Egypt, as one of the 'Two Ladies' udj.t -nkhb.t and the central role that the royal women fulfiled as incarnations of these

184

Two Ladies, is a subject treated in depth by Troy [8]; whose thesis is centred upon an identification of each royal Princess with the Cobra aspect of the Two Ladies, with the elder aspect of the Vulture-Goddess being associated with the Queen after childbirth and with the dowager-Queen. Thus, the secular role which these sovereign emblems have within Dynastic Egypt reveals their dual religious function - as symbolising the aspects of East (Cobra) and West (Vulture) that the" Mistress of the whole circuit of the solar disk" [6c] - the hm.t ntr fulfiled individually within her person in the course of her entire life.

That each subsequent Wife of Pharoah, literally the Wife of the God upon Earth, was also viewed as a direct incarnation of the Goddess Ast / Het-her emerges time and time again in closer examination of Temple and Tomb-reliefs and paintings. In this, Het-her outwardly appears as being the Goddess most intimately associated with the Queens of Egypt. An example of the Queen acting as the officiant in a ceremony to the Goddess is seen in the many beautiful paintings from the tomb of Nefer-ta-re, Rameses II' favourite wife and serves to dispel notions that women did not play an active role in Temple services. In one scene, Nefer-ta-re is portrayed before a heaped offering-table, presenting two nw-pots to the enthroned Goddess Hathor. The accompanying text says:

"hm.t nsw wr.t nb.t ns.y t3.y nb.t mr.t ns.y t3.y nfr-t3-re
rdit dt ti nn wr.t nhh mn r'
Ht-hr hr.t tp.t w3s nbt pt ntr.w nb.tw"

("The Queen (i.e Wife of the Sedge and the Bee) the Great Lady of the Two Lands,
the Lady greatly loved of the Two Lands, (in cartouche,Nefer-ta-re); addressing Het-her:
'Give life unto eternity & great eternal life, today; O Het-her Lady of the Sky foremost one
of power amongst the gods' ") [9]

The implication within this text and image, is that Het-her is the source of the life and power of the Queen and that the Queen was empowered within the official religion to directly invoke the Goddess' blessing on her own behalf, without recourse to a priest as intercessor. Images and texts such as this from within the mortuary Temples, also serve to dispel notions that the only religious functions women exercised with relation to Het-her were as royal-concubines, musicians, singers, or dancers.

With regard to Queen Nefer-ta-re, further wall-paintings and texts seem to offer a gender-fluid aspect to the Queen and her religious roles. A beautiful corner painting, bearing Nefer-ta-re' own cartouche displays a womanly-breasted, leopard-skinned priest with Cobra-diadem and accompanying text using feminine-t endings, walking towards an image of Osiris who has the feminine red-girdle bound about His waist. [10] (see: Appendix A).

The Queen officiating in the role of the Solar High-Priestess, imaged as Het-her, mother and wife of Horus as previously noted above; assists in obtaining a clearer perception, of perhaps,how easy the transition from a female role within the state religion to a male role, that is from a Solar High-Priestess, to a Solar High-Priest, may have been for any Queen to effect - for they contained the life and essence of the Sun. In this regard, Hatchepsut demonstrates the clear identification as an incarnation of the divine solar power which each Queen embodied and the dramatic manner in which the role of hm.t ntr could be transformed from being the 'Wife of the God' to being the god.

To place the transformation of Hatchepsut - from embodying a female role, to that of the supreme male role, as the incarnation of the Sun upon earth - as a female Horus of Gold - (i.e the Pharoah) into context, two points must be noted. Firstly, that the role of hm-t ntr was not limited to a High-Priestess incarnating the powers of the Celestial Cow-Goddess, Hether; the god Amun was noted as having a hm.t ntr by His side and many of the ntr.w had Wives and "earthly concubines" [(11)], who fulfiled both a secular and religious role, assigned to them:

"...namely Onuris, Harshef, Khons, Min, Sobk, Thoth, Iunmutef, and possibly Khunm of Hermopolis, and Upwawet of Asyut. It seems also probable that the "great noble ladies of the temple of Ptah " were regarded as Ptah's concubines, for the women who are presumably the concubines of Upwawet of Asyut are also designated "noble ladies".

"Strange to relate we even hear of concubines of certain goddesses with a presiding Chief of the Concubines in each case, namely Mut, Ubastet, Isis and Nekhbet. One cannot help thinking that the giving of earthly concubines to a god was no less a Heliopolitan institution than the giving to him of an earthly wife and musician-priestesses...the musician priestesses, also called Hathors, were...attached to the house of the God's Wife at Thebes." [(12)]

This is a central aspect of the role of women within the official religion of ancient Egypt in Dynastic times and particularly from the Middle Kingdom onwards, that women of high rank, selected from amongst the sisters and daughters of the royal household and then other notable families, were especially designated and appointed to fulfil this especially sacred and sexual office.

Until Roman times, certain religious rites within the Temple of Anubis were continued, in which the God visited his female devotees who took the offices of an "earthly concubine" in order to grant them special dreams and petitions. This ceremony was finally terminated after a Senator bribed one of the Priests who embodied Anubis, to allow him to take the Priest's place in the rite so that he could lay with a certain

Roman lady. The disrepute and sacrilege to this religious role that this act brought upon the temple, led to its destruction.

Amidst this well-established role, Hatchepsut, herself a formerhm.t ntr of Amun and mother of the Princess Neferure (13) assumed the full title and regalia of the King, following the death of her brother-husband, the Pharoah Thuthmosis 11. This left Hatchepsut in the position of no longer being the Wife of the God, but being the god and "as King needed a God's Wife to participate in the ritual aspects of her role and to ensure the preservation of maat " (14). It was the royal Princess Neferure who was designated and appointed to fulfil this office. A magnificent tomb-painting of Hatchepsut, shows her bearded and crowned with the twin plumes and horns of Her Father Amun and yet still robed in the dress of a woman (15) (see Appendix B) and further scenes from the so-called Chapelle -Rouge at Karnak depict Maat-k3-re and her hm.t ntr performing religious duties together, including "a ritual to destroy by burning the names of Egypt's enemies". (16)

This and other scenes emphasise that the role of hm.t-ntr encompassed the full spectrum of the Solar powers: that is both East and West, creation and destruction, as has been noted. That this role of the God's Wife was not merely a decorative accessory of the King, but fulfiled a purposeful and many-faceted role within the Egyptian religion and which had to be filled by a woman of the highest royal rank to ensure that maat was maintained, is a role within the ancient Egyptian religion most worthy of further investigation and documentation, beyond the scope of this essay.

Whilst only one woman could fulfil the role of the hm.t ntr in relation to any specific god at one time, the role itself being of a successive nature, with each Wife of the God holding her office for life and also designating who would follow her (in the absence of having a blood-daughter, appointing an adopted heir was accepted); there were roles of a lower rank within the official religion which were available to other women. Possibly the most numerous of these roles pertains to the musician-priestesses (hn.ywt; sm'.ywt) and the singers and dancers of each temple, judging from the numerous temple and tomb-paintings and reliefs which depict them in action. The instruments of music, small drum, tambourine and the sacred sisitrum and especially the voice, used so effectively in chanting and singing the songs and Hymn of Praise; filled the ancient Egyptian temples and palaces with pure joy. Evidence as to the divine nature of these female roles comes with the understanding that it is the Goddesses themselves who first perform the roles:

"Isis the Golden One...Isis the royal consort...Isis the bewigged, the Songstress...
Isis who greets the non-aggressor...Isis the living North Wind...
Isis in every place where Her k3 desires to be..." [17]

Those ritual objects particularly associated with the role and office of the priestess-musician were the sistrum, a hand-held rattle upon which the face of Het-her was depicted and the menit -collar. So sacred were these religious regalia and so closely identified were they with the Goddess Herself, that the possession and use of these objects within the context of a religious ritual, were deemed to be as if the divine Hathor was Herself present. The sistrum had a particular affinity with the removal, or banishing, of inappropriate influences within a ritual setting, rendering the place holy; whilst the menat had a complex association with a large sky-constellation of stars of the same name (no longer extant upon modern astronomical planispheres), portrayed upon the Denderah Zodiac and which contained the essence of Het-her, of use to invoke Her presence.

Numerous examples within temple and tomb-paintings and reliefs, as well as the vignettes accompanying the textual portions of *The Book of Going Forth By Day* [18] depict women officiating within a religious ritual and almost without exception are depicted holding (or wearing) these two powerful objects. Within *The Papyrus of Ani* [19], the royal Scribe Ani is shown accompanied by his Priestess-wife Tutu, "The Mistress Of The House, the Songstress Of Amun" [20] in sixteen of the thirty-seven vignettes. In each of these magnificient images, Tutu is portrayed holding the sacred sistrum and menat -collar; in addition, lotus flowers are held in and offered in several of the depictions. That Tutu's role was important, with regard to the religious rituals associated with Ani successfully negotiating his journey into the afterlife, is emphasised by her assisting Ani in certain of the key rituals of the text including: the Judgement Hall Scene (Plate 3); the prayers of approaching the Seven Gates of the Tuat (Plate 11) and the offering of Hymns of Praise to Osiris (Plates 2, 19, 30 etc). [21]

From temple and tomb-paintings and from the images of funerary papyri as discussed above numerous images of women depicted as musicians, dancers and the important role of 'Songstress' are extant. With regard to the role of 'Songstress', not only the Goddess Isis is renowned in this capacity and the songs and chants that were part of the official religion included both songs of joy, suitable for occasions such as births and marriages and also funerary dirges. In this latter role, two priestesses annually enacted the famous *'Lamentations of Isis and Nepthys'* to mark the murder of Osiris.

Isis and Her twin-sister Neb.t het ('Lady, or Mistress of the House') have an important animal transformation within the Egyptian otherworld as the Kite; a small hawk renowned for its screeching and which enabled the sisters to safely travel into the Tuat unobserved to effect the regeneration of Osiris. It is as 'Kites' that a class of paid women-mourners (dr.ty) played an important role within the funerary rites, in effect enacting the mourning of the divine sisters on a communal scale. The mourning of Isis and Nepthys was also annually enacted by two Priestesses who embodied the two Goddesses and was performed at the time of Osiris' murder accompanied by the annual Inundation of the Nile, viewed as the Goddess' tears. Part of these 'Lamentations' contain a direct reference to this time and the sorrow of the Goddess would undoubtedly have been felt by the two priestesses enacting these roles:

"Come quickly !... For I flood the Land with tears today;
My heart is hot at the wrongful separation
Yearning for the love that was lost;
I hid me in the bulrushes, to conceal the Child,
The Sun who would avenge His Father's wronging. (22)

The immense importance that the 'Songstress' had within religious rites lays with the fact that it was her songs, hymns and chants which accompanied the ritual gestures of the Priests and officiants in many instances and which were responsible for awakening the latent power of the actions, as well as heralding the immense and effulgent splendour of the divinity whom they served:

"'ir.i sss.w m hr.t nfr 'st di.t 'nhk hr.yt-ib 'I't-w'bt 'ir.t-r' iw.ty sn nw.t=s m pt t3."

("I play the sistra before your beautiful face, Ast, Giver of Life, residing in the sacred mound, Eye of Ra, who has no equal in the Sky or Earth.") (23)

Upon an examination of the primary sources, particularly the temple inscriptions and the tomb and funerary papyri of the Middle and New Kingdoms, down to the Ptolemaic times; the plethora of roles which women held within the official religion of ancient Egypt emerge as being well-defined by these times and of equivalent importance to the roles which men held, by comparison. From the youngest nubile dancer to the highest role of hm.t ntr, each aspect enacted by women served to support and to create the multifaceted aspects of the official religion and most importantly, to bring the essence of the ntr to earth. It is from contemplation of this latter role of hm.t ntr that evidence mounts in support of this thesis: that women were *of equal status within the official religion*; for in the final analysis,who can bring forth a God, but a God?

ENDNOTES

1. TROY, Lana *Patterns Of Queenship In Ancient Egyptian Myths and History*, Uppsala Press, Sweden, 1986. p. 10 section 1.5.
2. BLACKMAN, Aylward M. *"On the Position Of Women In The Ancient Egyptian Hierarchy"* (article, see Bibliography);
3. Ibid., p. 8.
4. Ibid., p.28.
5. ZABKAR, Louis V. *Hymns To Isis In Her Temple At Philae*, Brandeis University Press, University Press of New England, U.S.A., 1988. Hymn 3 p. 42.
6. (a), (b), (c), Blackman, p. 29.
7. HORNUNG, Erik Das Grab Des Horemheb, Francke Verlag Bern, Switzerland, 1971.
p.29; see charts Abb.5 & 6.
8. Troy, as per #1 above.
9. Tomb of Queen Nefertare, Dynasty XIX, Image from the Unesco World Art Series, published by the New York Graphic Society. Translation my own.
10. SADEA/SANSONI (Editori) *La Valle Dei Re e Delle Regine.*
11. BLACKMAN, p.16
12. Ibid., Italics as per Blackman.
13. TYLDESLEY, Joyce *Hatchepsut the Female Pharoah*, Viking Books, England, 1996. p.74 (Chart).
14. Ibid., p.89.
15. SADEA/SANSONI Plate of Tomb-Painting.
16. TYLDESLEY, p.89.
17. FAULKNER, Raymond O., *An Ancient Egyptian Book Of Hours*, (Pap. Brit. Mus. 10569), Griffith Institute At The University Press, Oxford, 1958. p.13, lines 18.19 - 19.5.

18. The term *The Book of Going Forth By Day* is used as it more accurately reflects the Middle Egyptian name of these funerary papyri (pr.t m hr.w) than the popular misnomer '*The Book of the Dead* '.

19. Ani was an XVIIth Dynasty Royal Scribe of the Gods whose funerary papyrus has been published several times this century as a '*Book of the Dead*'.

20. The official titulary of Tutu is in the text accompanying Plate 19 of the Faulkner, 1994 Edition.

21.Ibid., See 'Map Key To The Papyrus Of Ani' pp.94-97.

22. Modern rendering of *The Lamentations of Isis and Nepthys*.

23. ZABKAR, 1988. Hymn VII, pp.106-107; translation my own.

BIBLIOGRAPHY

BLACKMAN, Aylward M. *"On The Position Of Women In The Ancient Egyptian Hierarchy"* in *The Journal Of Egyptian Archaeology* Volume VII Parts I - II, April 1921, pp.8 - 30.

FAULKNER, Dr. Raymond O., *An Ancient Egyptian Book Of Hours*, Griffith Institute At the University Press, Oxford, 1958.

FAULKNER, Dr. Raymond O. & Goelet, Dr. Ogden *The Egyptian Book Of The Dead*, Chronicle Books, San Francisco, 1994.

HORNUNG, Erik *Das Grab Des Haremhab Im Tal Der Konige*, Francke Verlag Bern, Switzerland, 1971.

JUNKER, Hermann & Winter, *Erich Phila 1 & 2*, Der Osterreichischen Akadamie Der Wissenschaffen In Wien, Germany,1965.

JOHNSON, Sally B. *The Cobra Goddess Of Ancient Egypt*, Kegan Paul International, London, 1990.

NAVILLE, Edouard *Temple of Deir El Bahari: Part IV Hatchepsut & Shrine of Hathor: Part V Southern Hall of Offerings* Epigraphic Survey Volumes of the Egypt Exploration Society, England.

TYLDESLEY, Joyce Hatchepsut *The Female Pharoah*, Penguin Books, London, 1996.

TROY, Lana *Patterns Of Queenship In Ancient Egyptian Myths and History*, Uppsala Press, Sweden, 1986.

PLUTARCH, *De Iside et Osiride*, University of Wales Press, 1970. (J. Gwyn Griffiths ed. & trans.)

SADEA/SANSONI (Editori) *La Valle Dei Re e Delle Regine*.

ZABKAR, Louis V., *Hymns To Isis In Her Temple At Philae*, Brandeis University Press, University Press of New England, U.S.A., 1988.

FREE DETAILED CATALOGUE

Capall Bann is owned and run by people actively involved in many of the areas in which we publish. A detailed illustrated catalogue is available on request, SAE or International Postal Coupon appreciated. **Titles can be ordered direct from Capall Bann, post free in the** UK (cheque or PO with order) or from good bookshops and specialist outlets.

Do contact us for details on the latest releases at: **Capall Bann Publishing, Freshfields, Chieveley, Berks, RG20 8TF.** Titles include:

A Breath Behind Time, Terri Hector
Angels and Goddesses - Celtic Christianity & Paganism, M. Howard
Arthur - The Legend Unveiled, C Johnson & E Lung
Astrology The Inner Eye - A Guide in Everyday Language, E Smith
Auguries and Omens - The Magical Lore of Birds, Yvonne Aburrow
Asyniur - Womens Mysteries in the Northern Tradition, S McGrath
Begonnings - Geomancy, Builder's Rites & Electional Astrology in the
    European Tradition, Nigel Pennick
Between Earth and Sky, Julia Day
Book of the Veil , Peter Paddon
Caer Sidhe - Celtic Astrology and Astronomy, Vol 1, Michael Bayley
Caer Sidhe - Celtic Astrology and Astronomy, Vol 2 M Bayley
Call of the Horned Piper, Nigel Jackson
Cat's Company, Ann Walker
Celtic Faery Shamanism, Catrin James
Celtic Faery Shamanism - The Wisdom of the Otherworld, Catrin James
Celtic Lore & Druidic Ritual, Rhiannon Ryall
Celtic Sacifice - Pre Christian Ritual & Religion, Marion Pearce
Celtic Saints and the Glastonbury Zodiac, Mary Caine
Circle and the Square, Jack Gale
Compleat Vampyre - The Vampyre Shaman, Nigel Jackson
Creating Form From the Mist - The Wisdom of Women in Celtic Myth and
    Culture, Lynne Sinclair-Wood
Crystal Clear - A Guide to Quartz Crystal, Jennifer Dent
Crystal Doorways, Simon & Sue Lilly
Crossing the Borderlines - Guising, Masking & Ritual Animal Disguise in the
    European Tradition, Nigel Pennick
Dragons of the West, Nigel Pennick
Earth Dance - A Year of Pagan Rituals, Jan Brodie
Earth Harmony - Places of Power, Holiness & Healing, Nigel Pennick

Earth Magic, Margaret McArthur
Eildon Tree (The) Romany Language & Lore, Michael Hoadley
Enchanted Forest - The Magical Lore of Trees, Yvonne Aburrow
Eternal Priestess, Sage Weston
Eternally Yours Faithfully, Roy Radford & Evelyn Gregory
Everything You Always Wanted To Know About Your Body, But So Far
    Nobody's Been Able To Tell You, Chris Thomas & D Baker
Face of the Deep - Healing Body & Soul, Penny Allen
Fairies in the Irish Tradition, Molly Gowen
Familiars - Animal Powers of Britain, Anna Franklin
Fool's First Steps, (The) Chris Thomas
Forest Paths - Tree Divination, Brian Harrison, Ill. S. Rouse
From Past to Future Life, Dr Roger Webber
God Year, The, Nigel Pennick & Helen Field
Goddess on the Cross, Dr George Young
Goddess Year, The, Nigel Pennick & Helen Field
Goddesses, Guardians & Groves, Jack Gale
Handbook For Pagan Healers, Liz Joan
Handbook of Fairies, Ronan Coghlan
Healing Book, The, Chris Thomas and Diane Baker
Healing Homes, Jennifer Dent
Healing Journeys, Paul Williamson
Healing Stones, Sue Philips
Herb Craft - Shamanic & Ritual Use of Herbs, Lavender & Franklin
Hidden Heritage - Exploring Ancient Essex, Terry Johnson
Hub of the Wheel, Skytoucher
In Search of Herne the Hunter, Eric Fitch
Inner Celtia, Alan Richardson & David Annwn
Inner Mysteries of the Goths, Nigel Pennick
Inner Space Workbook - Develop Thru Tarot, C Summers & J Vayne
Intuitive Journey, Ann Walker Isis - African Queen, Akkadia Ford
Journey Home, The, Chris Thomas
Kecks, Keddles & Kesh - Celtic Lang & The Cog Almanac, Bayley
Language of the Psycards, Berenice
Legend of Robin Hood, The, Richard Rutherford-Moore
Lid Off the Cauldron, Patricia Crowther
Light From the Shadows - Modern Traditional Witchcraft, Gwyn
Living Tarot, Ann Walker
Lore of the Sacred Horse, Marion Davies
Lost Lands & Sunken Cities (2nd ed.), Nigel Pennick
Magic of Herbs - A Complete Home Herbal, Rhiannon Ryall
Magical Guardians - Exploring the Spirit and Nature of Trees, Philip Heselton
Magical History of the Horse, Janet Farrar & Virginia Russell
Magical Lore of Animals, Yvonne Aburrow
Magical Lore of Cats, Marion Davies
Magical Lore of Herbs, Marion Davies

Magick Without Peers, Ariadne Rainbird & David Rankine
Masks of Misrule - Horned God & His Cult in Europe, Nigel Jackson
Medicine For The Coming Age, Lisa Sand MD
Medium Rare - Reminiscences of a Clairvoyant, Muriel Renard
Menopause and the Emotions, Kathleen I Macpherson
Mind Massage - 60 Creative Visualisations, Marlene Maundrill
Mirrors of Magic - Evoking the Spirit of the Dewponds, P Heselton
Moon Mysteries, Jan Brodie
Mysteries of the Runes, Michael Howard
Mystic Life of Animals, Ann Walker
New Celtic Oracle The, Nigel Pennick & Nigel Jackson
Oracle of Geomancy, Nigel Pennick
Pagan Feasts - Seasonal Food for the 8 Festivals, Franklin & Phillips
Patchwork of Magic - Living in a Pagan World, Julia Day
Pathworking - A Practical Book of Guided Meditations, Pete Jennings
Personal Power, Anna Franklin
Pickingill Papers - The Origins of Gardnerian Wicca, Bill Liddell
Pillars of Tubal Cain, Nigel Jackson
Places of Pilgrimage and Healing, Adrian Cooper
Practical Divining, Richard Foord
Practical Meditation, Steve Hounsome
Practical Spirituality, Steve Hounsome
Psychic Self Defence - Real Solutions, Jan Brodie
Real Fairies, David Tame
Reality - How It Works & Why It Mostly Doesn't, Rik Dent
Romany Tapestry, Michael Houghton
Runic Astrology, Nigel Pennick
Sacred Animals, Gordon MacLellan
Sacred Celtic Animals, Marion Davies, Ill. Simon Rouse
Sacred Dorset - On the Path of the Dragon, Peter Knight
Sacred Grove - The Mysteries of the Forest, Yvonne Aburrow
Sacred Geometry, Nigel Pennick
Sacred Nature, Ancient Wisdom & Modern Meanings, A Cooper
Sacred Ring - Pagan Origins of British Folk Festivals, M. Howard
Season of Sorcery - On Becoming a Wisewoman, Poppy Palin
Seasonal Magic - Diary of a Village Witch, Paddy Slade
Secret Places of the Goddess, Philip Heselton
Secret Signs & Sigils, Nigel Pennick
Self Enlightenment, Mayan O'Brien
Spirits of the Air, Jaq D Hawkins
Spirits of the Earth, Jaq D Hawkins
Spirits of the Earth, Jaq D Hawkins
Stony Gaze, Investigating Celtic Heads John Billingsley
Stumbling Through the Undergrowth , Mark Kirwan-Heyhoe
Subterranean Kingdom, The, revised 2nd ed, Nigel Pennick
Symbols of Ancient Gods, Rhiannon Ryall

Talking to the Earth, Gordon MacLellan
Taming the Wolf - Full Moon Meditations, Steve Hounsome
Teachings of the Wisewomen, Rhiannon Ryall
The Other Kingdoms Speak, Helena Hawley
Tree: Essence of Healing, Simon & Sue Lilly
Tree: Essence, Spirit & Teacher, Simon & Sue Lilly
Through the Veil, Peter Paddon
    Torch and the Spear, Patrick Regan
Understanding Chaos Magic, Jaq D Hawkins
Vortex - The End of History, Mary Russell
Warp and Weft - In Search of the I-Ching, William de Fancourt
Warriors at the Edge of Time, Jan Fry
Water Witches, Tony Steele
Way of the Magus, Michael Howard
    Weaving a Web of Magic, Rhiannon Ryall
West Country Wicca, Rhiannon Ryall
Wildwitch - The Craft of the Natural Psychic, Poppy Palin
Wildwood King , Philip Kane
Witches of Oz, Matthew & Julia Philips
Wondrous Land - The Faery Faith of Ireland by Dr Kay Mullin
Working With the Merlin, Geoff Hughes
Your Talking Pet, Ann Walker
Menopausal Woman on the Run, Jaki da Costa
Environmental
Gardening For Wildlife Ron Wilson

FREE CATALOGUE
and
FREE MAGAZINE

Get a copy of our free detailed catalogue and register for your free* copies of *Inspiration* - the free Capall Bann magazine full of inspirational articles, reviews of music and books and news.

Just send your name and address to:

**Capall Bann Publishing
Freshfields
Chieveley
Berks
RG20 8TF**

* *Inspiration* is mailed out free within the UK, to have the magazine mailed overseas please send four IRCs. Our catalogue is sent out free worldwide.